Women's Voices
of Duty and Destiny

Speaking of Religion

Daniel S. Brown
Series Editor

Vol. 1

The Speaking of Religion series is part of the Peter Lang
Media and Communication list.
Every volume is peer reviewed and meets
the highest quality standards for content and production.

PETER LANG
New York • Bern • Berlin
Brussels • Vienna • Oxford • Warsaw

ADVANCE PRAISE FOR

Women's Voices of Duty and Destiny

"This book is inspiring and empowering for all women who struggle with the tension to uphold gendered, religious expectations and to pursue a calling to speak their convictions. The 14 remarkable women discussed in this brilliant book represent a wide range of faith traditions and demonstrate how women can reconcile this tension and thereby make immeasurable contributions to society, serving as exemplars for how we too can simultaneously fulfill our duty and our destiny." —DIANE M. BADZINSKI, PROFESSOR OF COMMUNICATION, COLORADO CHRISTIAN UNIVERSITY

"Kudos for a fresh collection of influential women's rhetoric! Elizabeth W. McLaughlin's book demonstrates the motivating power religious commitment has for shaping passionate speech. Her approach listens respectfully to the whole person in context, and she uses the narrative paradigm as a way of organizing her thoughts on women's religiously framed public address. The tension between duty and destiny, freedom and religious constraints pulls on the reader but is held together by the author's deep respect for women as image bearers of God. A worthy read!" —ANNALEE R. WARD, DIRECTOR OF THE WENDT CENTER FOR CHARACTER EDUCATION AND PROFESSOR OF COMMUNICATION, UNIVERSITY OF DUBUQUE

"Elizabeth W. McLaughlin's chosen speech artifacts deftly illustrate the push/pull tension of women extending our voices in championing peace, kindness, education, and spirituality all within the narrative space of women's positions in discursive communities. The topically arranged speeches in this volume bring forth the boundaries women are continually navigating regarding authority, scope of action, duty, and the notion that being female is 'not a blow' (Schlafly) from a variety of religious, social, and political perspectives. Together, the collection shines a much-needed light on universal and very human concerns as understood and articulated through women's voices." —MELINDA FARRINGTON, ASSISTANT PROFESSOR OF COMMUNICATION, SAINT VINCENT COLLEGE

"Elizabeth W. McLaughlin has compiled a valuable collection of women's speeches, many of which are not otherwise easily available. Although these texts span centuries, continents, and religious traditions, they sit at the intersection of religion and civic life and they consider humanity's most enduring questions of faith, freedom, relationships, and more. McLaughlin usefully elucidates the themes that run across the speeches, contextualizes each speaker and speech in its historical moment, and gives the reader critical vocabulary for interpreting each speech. The book makes these important speeches accessible to a broad audience." —KRISTJANA LYN MADDUX, ASSOCIATE PROFESSOR AND CO-DIRECTOR OF GRADUATE STUDIES, UNIVERSITY OF MARYLAND

"If there's a need for one thing in this age it is keen attention toward the significance of human personhood and dignity. Certainly, the crises facing our world are numerous, but as Elizabeth W. McLaughlin focuses the lens more narrowly on women's voices, a perspective is offered that has often been muffled—if not missing—in the history of oratory. The author's contribution to women's studies, religion, and the quest for meaning will be relevant and read for years to come." —STEPHANIE BENNETT, PROFESSOR OF COMMUNICATION AND MEDIA ECOLOGY AND FELLOW FOR STUDENT ENGAGEMENT, PALM BEACH ATLANTIC UNIVERSITY

"In few contexts have women's voices been more disadvantaged than in overtly religious ones. What makes this collection of public addresses by women particularly valuable is not just the illumination of the courage and determination of women to speak powerful and profitable words into the public and communal issues of their day, but also the power and importance of religious faith as a source of rhetorical invention. Elizabeth W. McLaughlin has assembled an engaging and heuristic array of speeches—some familiar, some less familiar, and some more counterintuitive—that collectively shows not only the insight and determination of women to be heard, but also their respect for the need to earn the right to be heard well by others that rhetorical theorists have emphasized from antiquity." —MARK ALLAN STEINER, ASSOCIATE PROFESSOR OF COMMUNICATION, CHRISTOPHER NEWPORT UNIVERSITY

"Elizabeth W. McLaughlin's well-written book exemplifies the tried and true 'text in context' approach to rhetorical analysis. Of course, by 'context' I mean each individual speaker's historical, philosophical, and societal context, not ours, no matter how much we are tempted to judge historical speakers and speeches according to our own contemporary ideas and standards. Furthermore, McLaughlin's book delivers to the reader glimpses of great women orators who did not dispatch or downplay their faith to become public figures, but brought their religious convictions into public life. In my opinion, there is an empty space on the shelf labeled 'Historical Speeches' where this book will proudly fit." —MICHAEL PHILLIP GRAVES, INDEPENDENT SCHOLAR

"Elizabeth W. McLaughlin states in her introduction 'the human desire to connect with the sacred is almost universal.' She then demonstrates an adept ability to connect her readers with feminine truth-seekers, holding hands across a vast expanse of time and place, bringing their concerns forward with fresh insight.

Against a contemporary societal mishmash of gender-bending dialogue, McLaughlin grounds us with a sincere consideration of worthy discourse that has stood the test of time. Using speech texts from an impressive array of mindful women from all walks of life and spiritual inclinations, she carefully examines a wide spectrum of communication perspectives and presents them objectively.

She provides circumstantial and individual personal context for each speech, thus lifting it above mere essay perusal. It's as if she has traveled far and wide to bring back a shipload of gems to share. After polishing them to expose the many facets, she provides the viewer glimpses into deeper prisms of truth.

Her articulate review of each speech text reveals her determination to explore the heart, mind and intuition of the speaker, while remaining true to her own role of honest examination. The work is both timely and provocative." —DARLENE GRAVES, PROFESSOR OF COMMUNICATION STUDIES, LIBERTY UNIVERSITY

"*Women's Voices of Duty and Destiny* is a 'must-have' addition to the bookshelf for any scholar of women's religious rhetoric. Elizabeth W. McLaughlin's book is a sensitive assessment of women's rhetorical contributions to numerous religious traditions. She doesn't shy away from including women, such as Phyllis Schlafly, whose rhetorical contributions do not fit into a traditional feminist canon, but who nonetheless did have a tremendous impact on feminist discourse and American politics." —CHRISTY MESAROS-WINCKLES, CHAIR COMMUNICATION ARTS AND SCIENCES, ADRIAN COLLEGE

Elizabeth W. McLaughlin

Women's Voices of Duty and Destiny

Religious Speeches Transcending Gender

PETER LANG
New York • Bern • Berlin
Brussels • Vienna • Oxford • Warsaw

Library of Congress Cataloging-in-Publication Data
Names: McLaughlin, Elizabeth W., author.
Title: Women's voices of duty and destiny: religious speeches
transcending gender / Elizabeth W. McLaughlin.
Description: 1 Edition. | New York: Peter Lang, 2019.
Series: Speaking of religion, vol. 1
ISSN 2575-9124 (print) | ISSN 2575-9132 (online)
Includes bibliographical references.
Identifiers: LCCN 2018035855 | ISBN 978-1-4331-5298-6 (hardback: alk. paper)
ISBN 978-1-4331-5297-9 (paperback: alk. paper) | ISBN 978-1-4331-5299-3 (ebook pdf)
ISBN 978-1-4331-5300-6 (epub) | ISBN 978-1-4331-5301-3 (mobi)
Subjects: LCSH: Women and religion—United States.
Social justice—United States.
Rhetoric—United States.
Classification: LCC HM671 .M39 2019 | DDC 200.820973—dc23
LC record available at https://lccn.loc.gov/2018035855
DOI 10.3726/b14853

Bibliographic information published by **Die Deutsche Nationalbibliothek**.
Die Deutsche Nationalbibliothek lists this publication in the "Deutsche
Nationalbibliografie"; detailed bibliographic data are available
on the Internet at http://dnb.d-nb.de/.

To all women who speak truth reflecting the image of the divine.

Table of Contents

Foreword

During the twentieth century a growing consensus emerged that there was a single canon of great speeches with which every student of communication should be familiar. At the dawn of the twenty-first century, however, Professor Martin Medhurst issued a call for a reconceptualization of the canon of public address when he wrote, "What can be done—and ought to be done—is for individual discourse communities to form their own canons through the process of rhetorical archaeology—the recovery of texts and discourses central to the self-understanding and public expression of specific groups and movements."[1] This is the precise call to which *Women's Voices of Duty and Destiny: Religious Speeches Transcending Gender* responds.

This volume is the inaugural contribution to Speaking of Religion book series. As a collection, the series grows from a scholarly attentiveness to the role that religion plays in the public sphere. The decline of religious influence in public affairs is a common yet false narrative in the United States. Americans remain a devout people who are motivated to action by their faith commitments. Several contemporary, interdisciplinary scholars point us toward the privilege that religion and faith enjoy in public life. Collectively their work asserts that the world has entered a post-secular era: Secularism is dead and God is alive.[2] As but a single example, Michael Minkenberg, writes about international policy debates and concludes that "even in the age of postmodernity, religion is still a force in the realm of politics, including policy making."[3]

The Speaking of Religion series features short books in response to Medhurst's call. These books focus on issues with which the public engages and in which religion is invoked. The author of each volume carefully curates a canon of authenticated speech texts that were either delivered by people of faith or were infused with religious arguments or a theological ethos. In most cases, the speech texts fulfill both of these criteria.

Professor Elizabeth W. McLaughlin herein focuses on religion and women. She identifies and investigates the tensions between the push women frequently experience between their *duty* to conform to pro-scribed women's roles and place, and the pull these same women experience towards *destiny* and human freedom. The dialectic that defines these women and their public discourse is animated by religious princi-ples. These are women who engage with the world on their own terms, demanding that they be respected while they likewise respect their lis-teners. To borrow W. Barnett Pearce's phrase, the speakers found in this volume are cosmopolitan communicators.[4] These are women of the world. They understand that their intellectual opponents were shaped by forces in the same way that they were shaped by political, religious, and social forces. And they understand the need for social eloquence, which is qualitatively different from rhetorical eloquence.

May we listen carefully and engage thoughtfully with their words, their dreams, and their ideals.

Daniel S. Brown, Jr., Ph.D.

Grove City, Pennsylvania

Notes

1. Martin. J. Medhurst, "The Contemporary Study of Public Address: Renewal, Recovery, and Reconfiguration," *Rhetoric & Public Affairs* 4, no. 3 (2001): 505.

2. One fine introduction to this theme is Peter L. Berger, *The Desecularization of the World: Resurgent Religion and World Politics* (Grand Rapids, MI: Eerdmans Publishing, 1999).

3. Michael Minkenberg, "Religion and Public Policy: Institutional, Cultural, and Political Impact on the Shaping of Abortion Policies in Western Democracies," *Comparative Political Studies* 35, no. 2, (2002): 243.

4. W. Barnett Pearce, *Communication and the Human Condition* (Carbondale, IL: Southern Illinois University Press, 1989).

Acknowledgements

It has been an extraordinary privilege to work on this collection of women's speeches, and many people have assisted in the making of this book. To all, I am grateful for your contribution, encouragement and guidance.

To Daniel S. Brown, Jr., book series editor, and Kathryn Harrison of Peter Lang Publishing, thank you for your patience with me in many questions and for the opportunity to work on this project.

To Agnes Baker Pilgrim, who reminded me to be grateful for every glass of clean water, and Dr. Brook Bello and Lana Pohlman of More Too Life for their inspiration to overcome life's challenges and stand up for what is right. Thanks also to human rights activist Jon Andrews for the introduction to Dr. Bello's work.

To Rabbi Sally J. Priesand who graciously agreed to let me include her words in this collection, and to Sr. M. Callisita from the Mother Teresa Center who went to the extra mile to find me in the midst of lost emails seeking help with Mother Teresa's speech.

To Deb Pentecost of the Phyllis Schlafly archive and Dr. Tasha Lucas Youmans of the Bethune-Cookman University Archive, thank you for your work in finding sources.

To Megan Clabbers, for her excellent advice, edits, friendship, and bringing order to chaos, and to Paige Comstock Cunningham, my best friend and role model, for excellent recommendations and ideas. Thank you.

To library director Janet Fore and the great women of the Cushwa-Leighton Library of St. Mary's College, Notre Dame, thank you for a welcoming, quiet place to think and write during my sabbatical.

To my colleagues at Bethel College, Indiana—Barbara Bellefeuille, Bradley Smith, Chad Meister, Marilee Crandon, and Brother Timothy Erdel—your ideas, recommendations, and support have been invaluable. To my students, I appreciate your encouragement and desire to change the world.

Finally, I thank my family—my husband Donald, daughters Kaitlin and Holly, sons-in-law Matthew and David, grandkids Owyn and Mia, and my dear Mother, Carolyn—for your patience and encouragement. You are my greatest joy.

All of you have made it possible for me to know more about what it means to bear the image of God, embody divine values, and to see the dignity of each person in the replenishment and restoration of the world.

Peace!

Elizabeth W. McLaughlin, Ph.D.

Mishawaka, Indiana

Introduction

"So, God created human beings in his own image. In the image of God, he created them; male and female he created them."

— Genesis 1:27, *New Living Translation*

"God is not feminine, but masculine. And man is made in the image of God. On the other hand, a woman is not made so much in the image of God, but in the image and as a mate to man."

— Rev. John R. Rice, "Bobbed Hair," Sword of the Lord Ministries

Before many faces, a woman approaches the front of a gathering intending to speak. Within their gaze, they consider who she is, why she is here, if she is worthy of attention, or if she even has the right to talk. Further, if she dares to connect her topic with any religiously inspired values, what gives her this authority? Is she forsaking her duty to conform to divine sanction, to community values, or is she fulfilling her possible calling to speak truth to power? Is it possible for a woman to connect to the divine, to speak from this perspective, and to claim authority with men to address the issues of her day?

These questions and dialectical tensions resonate through the words and witness of the women who speak throughout this book. As these opening quotations illustrate, women often experience the tension between the limits of gendered-duty and the promise of divine-human identity and dignity existing within many religions.

In many ways, this collection is a representative sample of women from all over the world, addressing injustices, calling for reform, and advocating for the common good. They embody a higher call for loving neighbor, reflecting their embodiment of the divine nature.

Women, public address, and religion—can these belong together? Many believe that religion silences women, opposes gender equality, and limits women's roles in life. This impression is understandable, but it is not the whole story. This study of women's voices starts with more profound questions about the role that religion plays in shaping the lives of individuals, families, communities, and nations. Whatever people believe—or do not believe about the nature of the divine—the human desire to connect with the sacred is almost universal. Religion's role in culture is highly contextual and an essential function of the social molding and defining process at all levels of human relations. Fundamental questions about the nature of human beings, how the world works, what human beings can and should do, how we relate to the divine, how gender and gender roles are defined, are all ways that religion impacts every aspect of life. While there is a growing animus toward organized religion, many still believe. According to a 2012 Pew Research study of 230 countries, eight-out-of-ten people in the world identify with a religious group.[1]

While this 80 percent figure reflects a dizzying array of religions and belief systems, it testifies to the enduring human search for the divine, for meaning beyond ourselves. Generalizations and stereotypes are dangerous when considering the complexity of women's lives and contexts. Some women live in the seamless center of their religion as part of their community and culture, while others may exist on the margins, with only a residual religious echo in their lives. Some religions are bound by sacred texts and their interpretations, while others lack a unifying set of beliefs. With its many complexities, sacred stories, cultures, and discourse communities, religion plays a central role in human life. And women, influenced by religious values, speak to change their world. This commitment to freedom frames this collection of speeches.

The two opening quotations illustrate the tensions, and competing narratives, women can experience in any religion. The first, found in Genesis the first book in the Hebrew and Christian scriptures, describes the divine creation of the world and human beings to bear this image. This passage frames the charge for woman and man to replenish and care for the creation as part of their shared destiny and purpose. In contrast, the second quotation from Christian fundamentalist John R. Rice, penned in the early 1940s, declares that women are not image-bearers, and interprets another biblical text to differentiate gender roles as a necessary duty to God. In this case, women cannot cut their hair and please God at the same time. In Rice's vision, and those of other religious fundamentalists continuing to this day, women are divinely decreed to marry, mother, cover, and submit, and in some cases, it is decreed that they cannot receive an education, drive a car, or even leave the house without male sanction. Further, in some contexts, women cannot testify in court, inherit, own property, or divorce. This tension between duty and destiny frames the lives of many women and girls, men and boys, as taught and practiced by their religious group, social group, and community.

Women speak, anyway, in the quest for dignity, equality, peace, and freedom.

Welcome to this exploration of 14 speech texts representing women from different religions, time periods, countries, and contexts. Some speakers are national or religious leaders, while others speak from their own experience of suffering and search for freedom. Each woman imparts the influence of her religious values as an explicit part of her public address. These are real women, in complex contexts, using their voices to influence others to consider their proposals to make society better for all people.

These speeches represent the many voices of women who speak with authority. While there are many differences between these speakers and speeches, they share at least five common characteristics.

First, they represent different religions, locations, and histories. These texts reflect Catholic and evangelical Christianity; Reformed Judaism; Buddhism; earth religion; and others.

Second, these speeches are not sermons to believers. While religious services can be open to the public, sermons are mostly directed to the faithful within a sacred context. On the other hand, public addresses includes speeches given to a mixed audience offered in a public, often civic forum, which concerns the lives of whole communities.

Third, each speaker uses explicit references to her religious faith and values to support her purpose to mixed audiences representing a discourse community in all its complexity. Using the principles of religion to argue for a position that may be opposed by many within that discourse community is an active rhetorical strategy.

Fourth, these speakers offer a rich variety of viewpoints on controversial issues, while seeing the connection with religious values. Two speakers might openly disagree about what is central to human freedom, as an example, without experiencing conflict in their shared religious perspective.

Finally, these speech texts demonstrate the dialectical tensions between the backward pull of duty and the forward push toward transcendent freedom and human destiny. Religion has the social power to constrain and limit while motivating believers to seek justice and better human flourishing. After selecting the speech texts, five themes emerged: faith, society, education, reform, human freedom, and peacemaking.

Terms and Definitions

While every effort has been made to avoid using obscure jargon in this book, some terms need explanation for better understanding. There are limitations and nuances that may not be covered in these definitions, but simplicity and clarity are the goals.

For example, the terms religion and spirituality are easy to confuse. For our purposes, *religion* includes any system of beliefs about the nature of the supernatural and divine, resulting in an organized set of practices and rituals shared by a group of people. This definition should encompass both traditions framed by sacred texts and those that are not. In many cases, these speech texts are addressing an audience with a shared cultural understanding of certain symbols, beliefs, and even textual references. *Spirituality*, on the other hand, often expresses individual understandings and practices of the divine separated from organized religion.

The term *discourse community* refers to any size group or community that shares a common purpose, goals, and language to communicate and interpret religious truths and practices. The idea of intertextuality, or shared knowledge and teaching from layered sources into a web of meaning, is common to these communities. By its very nature, then, this collection of speeches includes religious references using language that communicates to audience members who share a common understanding of stories, symbols, and terms, even if they are not believers.

Narrative, as I am using it, refers to both the form of a story and its contents. This term includes the structural elements of a story—with a beginning, middle, end, characters, conflict, and other conventions—and how they create identification with the speaker's purpose and audience.

The terms *speaker, rhetor, and orator* are used interchangeably to refer to the women whose voices we hear in these spoken texts. The use of rhetor implies that as a speaker she is crafting her words artfully and appropriately; the term orator refers to the eloquence of the speechmaker.

Finally, *public address* refers to the context, purpose, and setting that these speeches have in common. Each one is made before a broad audience, in a public or governmental forum, and is not given at a worship event.

A Personal Note

Every writer or speaker has a perspective; I need to share a little of my religious experience to frame this exploration honestly. I am a middle-aged, "middle-class" white woman who came of age within a conservative Christian tradition that demanded women's silence and obedience to male authority. Following the literal interpretation of the Bible and the narratives of roles, I learned that men lead, and women's duty necessitated becoming smaller to accommodate male authority.

Within this narrative, women had to become less so that men could be more: in faith, family, society, and life. I experienced a "double-bind"— or inner conflict about how to behave—within the competing stories about being a gendered, woman-person, while also a genuine believer with an urgent desire for a full life.

These competing stories have not only affected my personal and professional life, but also the lives of others. Women at the religious college where I teach have felt the call to serve in places where they have learned that they cannot because of their gender. While I recognize the many advantages of my life, free from the extremities of abuse and hardship, I have sought, both in lived experience and scholarship to understand what it means that women and men share the divine image together and how this can help build a better world. Through the filter of this life experience, I have identified texts that exemplify an answer to this compelling quest: understanding women's voices that transcend gender and call to a better destiny grounded in human dignity. To consider these speeches and their power, we must first briefly address the multifaceted, multilayered nature of women and religion.

Women and Religion

Women's lives have been impacted profoundly by religious traditions in shaping their roles, status, and lifestyles. It is impossible to isolate the practice of religion from the culture that surrounds it. Everyone lives in social groups from the immediate family, local community, and region to the nation and, in some cases, the world. Religious beliefs and practices exist in a complex web of relationships, identities, and circumstances, shaped by distinct discourse communities. For example, Muslim women in Tehran, Detroit, Tangiers, and Paris have vastly different experiences and expressions of their religion, just as Christians and Jews from New York and Moscow have theirs. While every religion has its stereotypic, fundamentalist practices limiting women, these stereotypes must not overshadow the rich variety and nuance of life in families, communities, and nations. Each woman inhabits and addresses audience members living inside and outside distinct discourse communities and groups. In looking for religion's implicit or explicit influences in each speech text, we must consider each orator's discourse communities, her place or role within these communities, whether she has chosen her religion or is a cultural participant, as well as how these dynamics exist in the diverse audiences she addresses.

Religious scholar Majella Franzmann offers a useful typology for each of these categories to situate this relational matrix as discourse communities. First, she describes women as participating in "natural" religious communities as those places where the experience of the group seamlessly blends or has "coterminous" identity. The life experience of the community includes the religious life for all.[2] Second, in "universalizing" communities, the experience of religion is local, while also having a strong global identity and presence.[3] Finally, "sectarian" groups are largely separated from the larger world.[4]

Women's experiences with their religion are also important factors to understanding the values she holds. Some of the speakers in this book are formal religious or world leaders, and others are part of the dominant values of cultural faith they share with their audiences. Other speech-makers witness from their own place of suffering in advocating for the voiceless. Each participant has her own personal faith journey of discovering what her religion means, or does not mean, in her life, practice, thinking, and activism. Additionally, each speaker carefully crafts her words for the discourse communities of her audience, including their religious perspectives.

Women as Public Speakers

Every public speaker must consider the importance of ethos, or his or her credibility and reputation about their topic, audience, purpose, and context. One must earn the right to be heard. This reputation depends on the rhetorical choices a speaker makes, what the audience knows about his or her life, the language used, the effectiveness of the delivery, and other factors. The central question is authority. Why should I listen to this person as an expert or storyteller? In many contexts, women's public address is suspect with her subordinate position in society, mainly involving any religious authority. Women who speak for change must often balance the perception of appropriate feminine traits with the stereotypic masculine task of oratory.

Every woman in this collection speaks from her own ethos, an authority based on real lived experience, textual appeals, storytelling, rhetorical skill, and some with the perceived "moral authority" of being a woman. Each orator grounds her speech from the moral authority of personal experience and offers her witness to justify the change she seeks. Several speakers appeal to their sacred texts for examples and principles supporting their appeals, and they also refer to "secular" texts such as the U.S. Declaration of Independence to connect their positions to the values of community and nation.

As storytellers, these speakers excel. With anecdotes from their own and others' lives, each one appeals to their audience's emotional needs (pathos) to illustrate the predicament they are addressing. These narratives invite the audience to participate in the solution to injustice and suffering. With vivid language and passion, this use of story is one of the many rhetorical skills these orators share. Some speakers effectively use the perception of women's superior moral authority to counter their opponents' arguments for the status quo. Each speaker commands her own authority by the way she lives and by what she invests into the lives of others.

What to Look for in Speech Analysis

When you hear a speech, how do you evaluate it? It probably depends on the circumstances surrounding the event and why you are present. If the topic is interesting and relevant, then you may listen differently than if you are required to attend. When reading speeches from the past, we remember that each one was initially an immediate event, for a specific place, context, and time. Understanding the circumstances birthing each address is central to interpreting its meanings and messages as juxtaposed with religion. The speeches in this book call for an in-depth look at the historical situations they represent.

Within this work, each themed section introduces a central idea present in each public address. Before each speech, a brief account of the rhetorical situation—speaker, purpose, audience, topic, and context—helps to position one's reading of the ideas the orator presents. The objective is to frame each speech and allow for further exploration and research of the speaker and her life situation.

While there are many worthy approaches for rhetorical speech analysis, Walter R. Fisher's narrative paradigm makes sense to frame public address and is appropriate for this book. In *Human Communication as Narration: Toward a Philosophy of Reason, Value, and Action*, Fisher posits that human beings are essentially tellers of stories and that the form of a narrative is universally understood. Women rhetors frequently use story as a vehicle for connecting with their audiences about difficult issues calling for change. Additionally, most religions depend on the telling and retelling of sacred stories to educate and inspire believers. This rhetorical approach fits this speech collection. The narrative paradigm offers the means to identify the values within a message, as well to examine their implications. Its approach practically aligns values with human action.

The narrative paradigm assumes several principles to understanding how its theory about story works. First, as previously discussed, Fisher has declared that humans are by nature storytellers.

Second, "human decision making and communication" are governed by "good reasons" that vary with the situation, media, and genre of the story.

Third, these "good reasons" are the product and practices formed within the context of history, culture, and biography.

Fourth, humans determine the rationality of a story by its *"narrative probability"* (Is the story coherent?) and by its *"narrative fidelity"* (Does it ring true?).

Finally, the fifth presupposition is that "the world as we know it is a set of stories that must be chosen among for us to live life in a process of continual recreation."[5] Fisher calls this narrative rationality universal and accessible to "all persons not mentally disabled." Almost all humans can make these judgments between stories because narrative "is a feature of human nature and…it crosses time and culture."[6]

For religious speeches transcending gender, then, audience members listen to each speaker and weigh the truth of the world she describes based on whether it holds together and how it compares to their experiences. Religious references, contexts, and texts weave together throughout these narratives. As Fisher explains, we are all continually choosing among conflicting stories and living by them, according to the logic of good reasons. For this collection, we will consider the "stories" each speaker offers from the dialectical tensions of duty and destiny; these tensions ask audience members to discern between the divine demand for duty and religion's higher call for human freedom. The reference to story or narrative includes the familiar elements and structures of this form which also coincides with the events of human life: a single day, the seasons of a single year, and the years of a human life.

Five components, Fisher has said, work together in the logic of good reasons. Each of these questions can apply to speeches and other texts:

1. Question of fact: What are the facts and values in this speech?
2. Question of relevance: Are the values appropriate to the decision in the message?
3. Question of consequence: What are the effects of these values for all affected?
4. Question of consistency: Are the values validated in real life?
5. Question of transcendency: Do these values represent "the ideal basis for human conduct"?[7]

This last question, the one of transcendent value, concerns those "ultimate values" that the speaker assumes are a given, those that reveal "one's most fundamental commitments."[8] Religious values are these kinds of transcendent values answering the most basic questions of the human condition. Each speaker deftly appeals to these values shared by her discourse communities.

The women speaking in this collection offer their visions or narratives of destiny against the backdrop of their contemporary religious and cultural narratives. For example, the opening quotations to this introduction tell two different stories about the creation and purpose of women. In the biblical account of Genesis 1, God creates man and woman in the divine image and charges them both with the replenishment and care of the earth. In this version, the *value* is equality of the sexes in freedom and responsibility, which is *relevant* to guide gender roles and relationships. *Equality is desirable* for human harmony and flourishing. In *real life, men and women do work* together to accomplish life's tasks. The *value of equality is transcendent* for human conduct.

In Rice's quotation, the story is presented differently. Based on Genesis 2, woman is created to serve man, who bears the divine image. Woman does not bear God's image separate from her relationship to the man. Her purpose is to serve the man in his image-bearing responsibilities. The *value* in this story is the supremacy of man and the subordination of woman; the message is for women to obey and help men. This view may be *desirable* to some and not to others. In *real life*, patriarchy permeates all levels of religion and society. Is women's subordination to men *transcendent and ideal*? In many religions, this subservient role centralizes woman's place in the cosmos as her divine duty. The women in this book, however, would say no. Combined they tell the story of a better world framed in the transcendent religious values of dignity and equality.

Themes and Speeches

The first section of this book, entitled "Faith," features two speakers who are recognized leaders in their religious communities. Each leader speaks with divine authority born of life experience, passion, and hard work to command respect among her people.

Rabbi Sally J. Priesand, the first woman ordained as a Reformed Rabbi, describes her early calling to lead a congregation, the discrimination she faced, the people who helped her, and the hard work she did to fulfill her dream. Her address "Reflections on My Life as a Rabbi," her acceptance speech for the Elizabeth Blackwell Award, expresses her purpose to participate in God's work of *tikkun olan*, or repairing the world.

Agnes Baker Pilgrim, leader of the Council of the Thirteen Grandmothers and eldest member of her people, also wants to repair the world through her global peacemaking effort. She calls on all people to recognize, heal, and appreciate the connection to all things in the Great

Mother. Her address, "Water," challenges her hearers to preserve and appreciate this life-blood and to share this message with others.

In the section, "Society," we hear the voices of three different women from different perspectives of women's place and responsibilities in the social order. All three speech-makers are from the United States and share a desire to improve women's lives but diverge on what this looks like.

Clarina Howard Nichols argues in her address, "The Responsibilities of a Woman," that for women to fulfill their divine calling within the home, they must have rights to education, inheritance, equal share in the marital property, and guardianship of their children upon a husband's passing. Her impassioned effort to change unjust laws is argued within the prescribed societal duties of her time.

In contrast, Phyllis Schlafly counter-proposes that women should retain their special status in society and shun efforts for equality with men in her address, "The Equal Rights Amendment (ERA)." Her campaign against the ERA successfully galvanized women to oppose this amendment to the U.S. Constitution, which narrowly failed passage in the 1970s.

Before the U.S. Congress, famous feminist and progenitor of *The Woman's Bible*, Elizabeth Cady Stanton, avers that, each woman is a solitary individual who must be responsible for herself as a person and a citizen before any of the roles she assumes. In this, women must have full rights to higher education and freedom for individual development.

In the section on "Education," two African American women speak on the importance of access to quality education as essential to the fulfillment of America's promise, from the strong motivation of the Bible and their Christian faith. Abolitionist Maria W. Stewart equates the dearth of educational options for African Americans to slavery in her 1832 address, "Why Sit Ye Here and Die?"

A little more than a century later, educator Mary McLeod Bethune echoes this same calling in her short radio address, "What Does American Democracy Means to Me?" She summons the audience to a spiritual awakening that connects the march to equality to a movement toward the light and fulfillment of the American Dream. Her references to the Bible and the Constitution foreshadow those made later by Dr. Martin Luther King, Jr.'s famous "I Have a Dream" speech.

In the section called "Reform," two religious leaders speak on the common issue of prohibition. The first address, "Everybody's War," features the fiery rhetoric of the president of the Women's Christian Temperance Union (WCTU), Francis E. Willard. Early in her career with the WCTU, Willard sets up the war on alcohol as a holy war between the forces of avaricious saloon owners and the virtuous goodness of Church, country, and family. In her time, she led the most successful women's organization in the nation.

In contrast is the short answer to the press by Aimee Semple McPherson, or simply "Sister Aimee." As a founder of a denomination, megachurch pastor, traveling evangelist, and roaring twenties celebrity, McPherson was a controversial and famous figure in the 1920s and 1930s. While scandal and disciples both followed her, McPherson speaks to the reality that human ideals and human behavior can contradict one another.

In the section entitled "Human Freedom," two voices speak against slavery and call for a greater commitment to the lives of women and girls. Both orators experienced the privations and suffering of slavery, one in the nineteenth century and the other in the twenty-first.

Sojourner Truth's classic address, "Ain't I a Woman?" contends from her plain speech that the argument against women's equality because of women's delicacy is ridiculous. Baring her arm to show her strength from ploughing the fields, Truth puts the audience to shame with the example of her life.

The next speaker calls her audience to action as well. Out of the experience of being abused as a young girl, Dr. Brook Bello advocates for change in laws and hearts to address modern-day sexual slavery. Bello has overcome her past and is an ordained minister, actor, filmmaker, and founder of the non-profit More Too Life. She personally lives what she advocates. Her address, "The Beautiful Color of Freedom." challenges all who listen to come up higher into getting involved for innocent children and realizing that there is more to life than the past.

The final section of this collection, "Peacemaking," features three internationally known speakers addressing their vision for a better world. While different in perspective and each widely criticized in public, each of these women has made important contributions to persons oppressed by poverty and governmental policy.

In this first address to the National Prayer Breakfast, Saint Mother Teresa of Calcutta claims that abortion as the greatest destroyer of peace contributes to the culture of death to her audience of politicians, pundits, and people of faith.

Dorothy Day, Roman Catholic socialist and activist, in this second address speaks up for five young men who burned their draft cards during the Vietnam War in her "Union Square Speech." As a radical Christian, she equates her passion to follow Christ with her Catholic pacifism and deep dedication to the poor.

The final speaker is Aung San Suu Kyi, affectionately known as "The Lady" to her people. Her life-long efforts to bring greater freedom to Myanmar (Burma), including the denial of her election to parliament by the Military, and later twelve-year house arrest, led the Nobel Committee to grant her the Nobel Peace Prize in 1991. Finally, in 2012, she was able to give her acceptance speech. In it she calls for greater peace and the practice of kindness, as inspired by her Buddhist religion.

This collection is certainly not exhaustive, but merely representative of the many women, throughout history, who have called for greater human dignity based on faith-inspired values. May they continue to rise and speak for generations to come.

Notes

1 "The Global Religious Landscape," Pew Research Center, December 18, 2012, http://www.pewforum.org/2012/12/18/global-religious-landscape-exec/

2 Majella Franzmann, *Women and Religion* (New York, NY: Oxford University Press, 2000), 41.

3 Ibid., 44–45.

4 Ibid., 47–48.

5 Walter R. Fisher, *Human Communication as Narration: Toward a Philosophy of Reason, Value, and Action* (Columbia, SC: University of South Carolina, 1989), 5; 64–66.

6 Ibid., 65–66.

7 Ibid., 108–109.

8 Ibid., 109.

Faith

Can a woman properly serve as the spiritual leader for her religious community and speak divine wisdom to her people? The answers vary with the sacred stories, culture, and changing histories that shape the narratives of religion. In the world's major religions descending from Abrahamic faith, the answer is traditionally no, with a handful of exceptions. Organized religion is historically patriarchal, with male leadership, hierarchies, and chains of command. Sacred texts, their interpretations and culture, often undergird prohibitions on women's leadership.

According to most in Jewish and Christian traditions, for example, the sin of Eve in Genesis grounds the eternal subordination of women as punishment (Genesis 3:16). In many communities, women are even forbidden to speak from a platform or teach when men are present. Islam, Hinduism, Confucianism, and others are notably patriarchal. Other religious traditions, however, are historically more egalitarian. Two examples are the Iroquois and Cherokee nations of North America as women served as clan leaders and performed sacred rituals.

Today, a growing number of women lead their churches, synagogues, and places of worship—but they are not without their critics. Advances for women in business, education, and society have generally been realized more slowly in religion. However, while some fundamentalist groups still limit women's roles, women as spiritual representatives are becoming a quotidian reality. The two speeches in this section reflect different traditions and different paths. These women share a commitment to translate their religious beliefs into action. One is from a religion that has traditionally opposed women as senior leaders, while the other has long recognized the wisdom of women. Each of these speakers has earned the respect of her discourse community through a lifetime of service.

Rabbi Sally J. Priesand, the first female rabbi ordained by a seminary in the United States, offers her acceptance speech for the Elizabeth Blackwell Award. In this presentation, the speaker tells her story about the joys and challenges she has faced over her career and offers parting wisdom to the college audience. Priesand's singular dedication to the hard work of becoming a rabbi inspires a generation of women to rise into leadership. Priesand's address appeals to the transcendent values of fairness, equality, hard work, and service to God and others.

In the second speech, Agnes Baker Pilgrim, chair for the Thirteen Indigenous Grandmothers, describes her love of Mother Earth and nature as being a whole that humans must care for and preserve. As a respected elder, she has traveled the world with her message of the sacramentality of all living things. This address, "Water," is a call to action for her listeners to wake up and realize the need to save waterways while there is still time. A spiritual leader of global influence, "Mother Aggie" calls all people to the transcendent values of stewardship and sacred connection to the earth and to all of humankind.

Rabbi Sally J. Priesand (1946–)

"When I decided to study for the rabbinate, I never thought much about being a pioneer, nor was it my intention to champion the rights of women. I just wanted to be a rabbi."

The path for women seeking to fulfill their call to spiritual leadership can be filled with steep hills and winding detours. Some enterprising women simply seek to serve without fanfare and succeed through sheer commitment and determination. Rabbi Sally J. Priesand, the first female rabbi to be ordained by an official seminary, is one who forged a path in her own journey to lead. Born in 1946, Priesand was encouraged by her parents to grow and become anything she wanted to be. In 1962, she decided that she wanted to be a rabbi and serve in a congregation.

Despite the resistance she faced, Priesand was the first woman at Hebrew Union College to complete the ordination process, and ordination followed in 1972. She served at the Stephen Wise Free Synagogue in New York as an associate rabbi; then, later assisted Temple Bethel-el in New Jersey and as a hospital chaplain. Rabbi Priesand finally found her home congregation in the people of Monmouth Reform Temple, Tinton, New Jersey, where she remained for twenty-five years. While she has accomplished much in her life, Rabbi Priesand humbly acknowledges her role is not as "the first female rabbi," but rather says, "I'm just the rabbi."[1]

This presentation is Priesand's 2009 acceptance speech of the Elizabeth Blackwell Award from Hobart and William Smith Colleges, separate institutions for men and women who "perform outstanding service to humankind." She begins her address noting the similarities between Blackwell[2] and herself: born in Cincinnati, Ohio, encouraged by family, supported by educators, and affirmed by male classmates in being the first women in their professions. This identification with Blackwell fixes Priesand's ethos as an award recipient and connection with the occasion.

Priesand's speech is organized topically in three sections—her own story of becoming a rabbi, results she sees from the unfolding of Jewish feminism, and "a few words gleaned from the challenges I've faced." Her language is plain and straightforward, adding to her ethos as a teacher. She is very open about her life circumstances, professional challenges, battles with cancer, and her desire to be simply a rabbi, a teacher of Judaism. "[Life] is not measured by wealth or power, material possessions or fame. Life is counted in terms of goodness and growth."

Through her faith, Priesand has inspired other women to take up the mantle of leadership.

* * *

"Reflections on My Life as a Rabbi" (2009)[3]

Hobart and William Smith Colleges

Geneva, New York

April 23, 2009

Thanks so much for that gracious introduction and for the very warm welcome you have afforded me today. I have enjoyed the beauty of your campus, the opportunity to meet with faculty, students and President Gearan, the kindness of so many staff members as well as the hospitality of Hillel and the wonderful Abbe Center for Jewish life. It is obvious to me in this very short visit that Hobart and William Smith Colleges reflect a unique atmosphere of intimacy and pride that other centers of higher education would do well to imitate. I am honored to receive an award that over the years has been presented to so many truly distinguished women. In preparing to speak to you tonight, I did some research on the life of Elizabeth Blackwell and was startled to see how many similarities there were between her journey and my own. She lived in Cincinnati and so did I. Her family supported her decision to do something a woman had never done before and so did mine. She was encouraged by some to become a nurse instead of a doctor, and I was toward the field of religious educations. She had the support of a man named Joseph Warrington, a well-respected physician in Philadelphia, and I had the support of a man named Nelson Glueck, distinguished archeologist and president of the Hebrew Union College–Jewish Institute of Religion.

When the male students at Geneva College were asked to vote on her admission, it was reported that "the whole class arose and voted 'Aye' with waving handkerchiefs, throwing up of hats, and all manner of vocal demonstrations." When I was called forward to be ordained, my classmates, 35 men, all rose spontaneously to honor this break-through in Jewish history—a memory that I very much cherish. When Geneva's Dean spoke at Elizabeth Blackwell's graduation, he congrat-ulated her on her diploma and expressed "admiration at the heroism displayed, and sympathy for the sufferings voluntarily assumed." One of my classmates spoke and said: "Rabbi Sally graced our class during those trying years," and Dr. Alfred Gottschalk who ordained me said he was doing so with "pride, dignity and pleasure."

Elizabeth Blackwell's story is now part of the rich legacy of this institution, never to be forgotten because of the granting of this award, and I am proud that the Hebrew Union College–Jewish Institute of Reli-gion has a chair in Jewish Women's studies that bears my name. Many similarities between our two journeys, and I thank you for the opportu-nity to discover that and to share with you this evening my own story which I have divided into three parts: first, I would like to tell you a little bit about myself and the journey that led me to the rabbinate; sec-ondly, share with you a few reflections on some of the changes I have witnessed in the religious community as a direct result of feminism, and finally, a few words gleaned from the challenges I have faced.

I decided I wanted to be a rabbi when I was 16 years-old, way back in 1962. Unfortunately, I do not remember why. I do remember always wanting to be a teacher, and whatever my favorite subject was at a particular time was what I was going to teach. One year, I dreamed of being a math teacher, and the next, a teacher of English, or perhaps French. In the end, I decided to be a teacher of Judaism, which is what a rabbi really is.

Fortunately, for me, my parents gave me one of the greatest gifts a parent can give to a child: the courage to dare and to dream. As a result, I remained focused on my goal, unconcerned that no woman had ever been ordained rabbi by a theological seminary and determined to suc-ceed despite the doubts I heard expressed in the organized Jewish com-munity. In those days, I did not think very much about being a pioneer, nor was it my intention to champion the rights of women. I just wanted to be a rabbi.

Although my parents were actively involved in Jewish organizational life, my family was not particularly observant. We did light Shabbat candles, celebrate Chanukah with our extended family and have a Passover Seder to which each of my siblings and I were encouraged to invite a non-Jewish friend to share the festivities and learn more about Judaism. I can still see my father at the head of our table, reclining on his pillow, leaving the table at the appropriate time to wash his hands, explaining the symbols on the Seder plate and reading every word of the Haggadah. My mother, of course, had been preparing for days, making gefilte fish from scratch and fashioning those delicious matza balls that were especially light and fluffy.

One year, my father's business brought him into contact with a Catholic children's home run by a group of nuns. Passover was approaching, and in the course of conversation, the Mother Superior began asking questions about the customs and traditions of this holiday. Before long, my father had offered to conduct a Seder for 52 nuns (and the Monsignor!), volunteering my mother, of course, to oversee the meal and make enough chicken soup and matza balls for all the participants. My father read the Haggadah, and the youngest nun recited the Four Questions. My mother still remembers entering the dining room on the day of the Seder and being greeted by a huge sign that simply said "Shalom." Moreover, the nuns presented her with a beautiful two-tiered silver tray that we continue to cherish.

My father died in 1968. I will never forget the kindness of the nuns who, dressed in their traditional garb, came to our home while we were sitting Shiva to remember my father and give thanks for his life—and I am ever grateful to my parents for teaching us by example that all people are God's children and we have much to learn from each other.

As soon as I began to express more than a passing interest in our religious heritage, my parents made certain to include among my birthday or Chanukah presents more Jewish books, often inscribed by my father with a few words of encouragement, a wonderful way to help me expand my horizons and at the same time validate the seriousness of my intention.

I grew up in the suburbs of Cleveland, and when I was in the eighth grade, my family moved from the east side of town to the west. As a result, my teenage years were spent in a predominantly non-Jewish neighborhood. In fact, my brothers and I were the only Jews in our high school. That made our participation in religious school and youth group all the more essential. We were active members of Beth Israel–The West Temple, a small congregation that taught me important lessons about what it means to be a temple family and how central to Jewish life is the task of *tikkun olam*, repairing the world. Although I did not become Bat Mitzvah, I was confirmed and continued my religious school education through the twelfth grade.

One summer, I was scheduled to go to the Girl Scout Roundup in Colorado, but my congregation awarded me a scholarship for what was then called the Union Camp Institute in Zionsville, Indiana, one of numerous camps in North America sponsored by the Union for Reform Judaism. Looking back now, I know that was a tipping point in my life. I was so honored that my congregation wanted me to represent them that I could not say no. It was a wonderful summer, and I came home with renewed enthusiasm and an even greater desire to share my love of Jewish tradition. So, I always tell people that for $100, my congregation received in return a lifelong commitment to Judaism and the Jewish people.

As the time for college approached, my desire to be a teacher of Judaism remained firm, and I knew that for me the best way to accomplish that goal was a career in the rabbinate. I applied to the Undergraduate Program jointly sponsored by the University of Cincinnati and the Hebrew Union College–Jewish Institute of Religion. I was accepted, and in 1964, I began my studies. My years in rabbinic school were fraught with challenge. Some members of the college community thought I came to marry a rabbi rather than be one, and my sincerity was often suspect. Consequently, I was under constant pressure to prove myself. Always I felt the need to be better and do better than my classmates so that my commitment and my academic ability would not be questioned. Occasionally, I sensed that some people would not be overly upset if I failed. More than once it would have been easy to drop out, but I persevered because I truly wanted to be a teacher of Torah.

Happily, I had the support of Dr. Nelson Glueck, at the time president of the College Institute who gave me his unqualified support and took care of a lot of little problems in the background that I probably never even knew about. Unfortunately, he died the year before I was ordained, but his wife Helen, a distinguished physician in her own right, told me that prior to his death he said there were three things he wanted to live to do and one of them was to ordain me. His vision and commitment laid the foundation for the ordination of women—and fortunately for me, Dr. Alfred Gottschalk shared that vision, and when he became president of the College–Institute, he made the dream a reality by ordaining me on June 3, 1972, together with the 35 men who were my classmates. Finding a job was not that easy. Some congregations wanted me for my publicity value to be able to say they were the first to hire a female rabbi, and others would not talk to meet at all.

In the end, I was the last person in my class to get a job, but in my opinion, I got the best job of all—assistant rabbi at Stephen Wise Free Synagogue in New York City. It always seemed particularly appropriate to me that I would come to a synagogue with a reputation for commitment to equality and social justice. Rabbi Edward E. Klein always took great pride in being introduced as the first equal opportunity employer in the American rabbinate.

I stayed at the Free Synagogue for seven years, and to be honest the circumstances under which I left were not all that pleasant. I hoped I would be given a chance at some point to be the senior rabbi but that was not to be. Neither that synagogue nor any other was ready nor willing to grant the title of Senior Rabbi to a woman. Indeed, for two years I was unable to find a full-time position. I served as a chaplain at Lenox Hill Hospital in New York City and accepted a part-time position at Temple Beth El in Elizabeth, New Jersey, a synagogue of older members who were always warm and welcoming.

In 1981, I became rabbi of Monmouth Reform Temple in Tinton Falls, New Jersey, a position I was privileged to hold for 25 years. The decision to retire three years ago was my own, believing as I do that rabbis—and a lot of other people—should know when to leave. It is always wise to say goodbye when people still like you. I did choose, however, to remain in my community and, as Rabbi Emerita, I worship at my temple every week, enjoying as I do the view from the pew.

I have never regretted my decision to enter the rabbinate, and clearly my life has been enriched by the people I have been privileged to serve these past four decades. One of the reasons I did so enjoy being a congregational rabbi was the opportunity to read Torah aloud from the *bima* at services and explore with my congregants the meaning of the text. Whenever I do that, I remember Sinai, the central event in the history of the Jewish people when we made God's law our own. I also recall a special moment in my life, one that happened just prior to my ordination as rabbi.

The ceremony of ordination is a public event, but it was preceded two days before by a private ceremony held in the chapel of Hebrew Union College in which each member of my class was handed the Torah scroll by Dr. Gottschalk. Individually, one by one, we received Torah, and while holding it close to our hearts, we affirmed our commitment to the values it represents and our desire to serve God and the Jewish people. It was a powerful moment for me, in some ways more mean-ingful than the actual ceremony of ordination. I have never forgotten it, and over the years, whenever I read Torah, study it, or simply take it from the Ark, I feel as if I am receiving it anew.

At that time, we were also asked to say a few words about our own personal philosophy. I quoted a verse from *Pirke Avot*, that tractate of the Talmud that contains the spiritual wisdom of the Jewish people: in Hebrew *emor m'aht va-asay har-bay*—say little and do much—it is a verse to which I have returned time and again throughout my rabbinate, believing as I do that our deeds speak louder than our words and truly reflect the beliefs we profess.

I am grateful to God that part of my life's work has been to open new doors for women in the Jewish community, but at the same time, I have tried never to lose sight of the larger mission of the Jewish people, which is to derive from the words of Torah a set of values and a sense of holiness that will enable us always to be partners with God in completing the world. What that means from my vantage point is not only participating in the task of *tikkun olam*, repairing the world, but creating a society based on equality and inclusivity, remembering that all of us are God's children, and as such, we should all have the opportunity to fulfill our creative potential to the fullest. My rabbinate has been based on the concept of empowerment. My primary task has always been to be a teacher of Judaism and help others become more responsible for their own Jewishness. It has not been my role to be Jewish for the sake of the congregation but to suggest ways in which all of us can be Jewish together.

In other words, rabbis are not surrogate Jews whose power is absolute, but facilitators and teachers who help others discover the richness of our heritage. In this realm, Jewish feminism has served as catalyst, encouraging us to rethink previous models of leadership in which the rabbi maintained complete control and did everything for members of the congregation. As pointed by Carol Gilligan and others, women are much more likely to engage in networking and partnership when relating to others.

Another area in which we see the impact of feminism is that of theology. Like most of you, I too grew up with the image of God as King, omnipotent and clearly male. My congregation gave me the opportunity, through experience and study, discussion and experimentation, to discover new models of divinity, to know that God embodies characteristics both masculine and feminine, to fashion for myself, and hopefully for them, a meaningful theology that has been a source of strength, particularly in those moments when it seems that we have used up all our strength. Together we have opened our hearts and our lives to greater spirituality. We have learned how to talk to God and with God rather than about God, to enjoy that intimacy that comes when addressing God as "You", knowing that every person should have the freedom to imagine God in any way he or she finds meaningful and satisfying. In many ways, Jewish feminism has been a grassroots movement and, therefore, change at the top has taken longer, but even there, tokenism is becoming a thing of the past. Over the past few years, nearly 30 women, all of them respected scholars, have joined the faculty of Hebrew Union College–Jewish Institute of Religion (an incredible accomplishment considering the fact that when I was a student there were no women on the faculty!), more women have become regional directors and vice chairs of the Union for Reform Judaism, and last month the Central Conference of American Rabbis installed its second female president. This bodes well for the future.

Surely one of the most powerful lessons we have learned from the Civil Rights movement is that if you do not see someone who looks like you in a position of leadership, then you begin to feel left out; you have a sense that it cannot be done. We teach our daughters and our sons that everything is possible, there are no limits on what they can achieve when seeking to fulfill their creative potential and contribute to the vitality of our country, but sometimes when they interact with large impersonal institutions, they discover a different message: a reluctance on the part of some to believe that women are as competent as capable as men. For decades now, we have been trying to change that attitude in every field of endeavor—medicine, law, accounting, education, even politics—and still we are engaged in the struggle to make certain that our daughters and granddaughters can be whatever they want to be, that they have not only equal opportunity but equal pay and that they are free from all forms of sexual harassment.

My life as a rabbi has also taught me something about the meaning of success. When I was first ordained, I thought the ultimate goal was to become rabbi of a large congregation; indeed, as the first woman to be ordained I thought it was my obligation. In so many different ways we are taught that bigger is better, but in reality, life is not measured by wealth or power, material possessions or fame. Life is counted in terms of goodness and growth. Someone once said that our purpose in living is not to get ahead of other people, but to get ahead of ourselves, always to play a better game of life. That is what success is all about.

Have we done our best?

Are we continuing to grow?

Are we affected more deeply today by love and beauty and joy than we were yesterday?

Are we more sensitive and compassionate to others?

Have we learned to overcome our fears and accept our failures?

Have we triumphed over selfishness and bitterness, cruelty and hatred?

Do we count our blessings in such a way that we make our blessings count? That is success. In the words of Albert Schweitzer: "The great secret of success is to go through life as a person who never gets used up. Grow into your ideals so that life can never rob you of them."

One final area in which Jewish feminism has made an important contribution is that of role models. We have begun to hear the stories of those whose voices have been silenced for too long, the countless numbers of women who have enriched the world from biblical times on. You may, for example, think that the ordination of women as rabbis is a relatively new idea. That is not true, and noted historian, Pamela Nadell, has shown otherwise in her fascinating volume, *Women Who Would Be Rabbis: A History of Women's Ordination 1889–1985*[4]. I highly recommend it for those who want to know more about the women who laid the foundation for my own ordination as rabbi. I also want to draw your attention to a wonderful exhibit about Jewish women that you can access online by going to the Web site of the Jewish Women's Archive—you will find copies of the original letters sent to me by the Hebrew Union College–Jewish Institute of Religion when I applied for admission.

Historically speaking, I am the first woman in the world to be ordained rabbi by a theological seminary, but on occasions such as this, I always like to give credit to the woman who was really the first woman rabbi. Her name was Regina Jonas. She finished her theological studies at the Berlin Academy for the Science of Judaism in the mid-1930s. Her thesis subject was "Can a Woman Become a Rabbi?" and naturally she set out to prove the affirmative. The faculty accepted her dissertation, but the professor of Talmud, the licensing authority, refused to ordain her. But Rabbi Max Dieneman, of Offenbach, did so privately, and she practiced until 1940, primarily in homes for the elderly. The Germans then dispatched her to the concentration camp at Theresienstadt, and she later died in Auschwitz. I would like to think that whenever people gather to hear my story our very presence brings honor to her memory.

One of the questions people most often ask me is: what is the most difficult thing about being a rabbi? For me, it has always been the need to change emotions at a moment's notice. For example, it is not unusual for a rabbi to celebrate a Bar Mitzvah and a baby naming, a funeral, a wedding and a round of hospital visits all on the same weekend. Each moment requires its own emotional investment, and a rabbi must be able to move from sadness to joy and often back again—and all this despite whatever may be going on in the rabbi's personal life at any given moment in time. Stress is a very real component of every rabbi's life, and every rabbi has to find his or her own way of dealing with it. For me, I decided to start painting—abstract watercolor—and it has become a wonderful way to calm my spirit.

I chose abstract watercolor for various reasons. First of all, I draw like I sing; in other words, I cannot even draw a stick figure. Second, to paint with watercolor does not require a lot of equipment and you can express yourself quickly and with relative ease. Third, the vibrancy of the color never fails to lift one's spirits. And finally, watercolor allows for spontaneity and the sheer joy of allowing the paint to have a mind of its own and do what it will. In this, we find the paradox of my personality. In most things, I am controlled and super-organized, but the abstract watercolor gives expression to the other part of me, the playful side. Rarely does a painting turn out the way I planned it in my mind, but that does not upset me in the least because I have so much fun matching wits with the paints as my brush glides across the surface of the paper, allowing me to bask in the brightness of the color and ultimately give thanks to God for implanting within each of us a spark of creativity.

Whenever we embrace that spark, we enrich life for ourselves and those around us. Now if truth be told I am a self-taught artist, enjoying the opportunity to experiment and discover new things on my own, learning by doing and enjoying the chance to listen to my heart and allow it to lead me wherever it will. I have heard it said that aspiring artists have a painting they see in their mind's eye. I am still in the process of trying to discover that painting and I am having an awful lot of fun doing it.

I first started painting when I was recuperating from a bout with cancer. As some of you may know, I have had cancer three times. Now I have read about people who have responded to such a challenge by saying "cancer was the best thing that ever happened to me." Personally, I have always thought that a rather strange thing to say. Although serious illness of any kind does come with its lessons—a reminder that each day is precious, that no life is free of difficulty, that priorities change as goals should be re-evaluated from time to time, that God walks with us wherever we go, that family and friends can help us over the rough spots if we let them—I would much rather learn these lessons another way, and I suspect you would too. Nonetheless, my bouts with breast and thyroid cancer did teach me a few things.

First, healing is hard work, but having a positive attitude helps. There are many things in life we cannot control, but how we respond to moments of challenge is something we can and do choose. Not long ago, someone asked me how can I continue to be so positive. I answered: it comes with my blood type (you guessed it—B+). A tongue-in-cheek answer for a serious question, but the fact is that holding on to our sense of humor is one way we defeat despair and maintain control over life's circumstances. "A joyful heart is good medicine," says the Bible, "but a depressed spirit dries up the bones" (Proverbs 17:22). Laughter puts life in perspective and helps us heal by enabling us, if even for a few moments, to release the anxiety that burdens our souls and forget the chaos that invades our world whenever illness strikes.

Second, a new insight for me was the realization that pets are very therapeutic. They give unconditional love and accept us as we are, no matter how we feel. Nearly seven years ago, just before my most recent bout with cancer, I acquired a 12-week-old puppy, a Boston terrier named Shadow. Throughout the weeks of treatment and recuperation, Shadow was by my side; indeed many a day was spent curled up on the couch together. He has proven to be a wonderful companion and a source of great amusement. He is cuddly and cute, has more toys than you can imagine, and his antics always make me laugh, no matter how tired I may feel—and yes, I will admit that he is as spoiled as any animal could possibly be!

The third thing I learned is that prayer makes a difference, both personal prayer and collective prayer. Asking God for the courage to cope with whatever the future may hold, for the wisdom to remain as even-tempered as possible despite being afraid or in pain, for patience and perseverance and the ability to endure a little more—asking God for all these things and knowing that God hears our words of prayer— was, and is, for me an enormous source of strength. How comforting it was to know that so many others were praying for me as well. Never underestimate the power of prayer. It may not lead to an instant cure, or even change a situation, but it does give us an opportunity to do something on behalf of those we love, especially at those times when we feel so helpless and fear there is nothing left to do. Praying for another person, and telling him or her about it, lets that person know that he or she has not been forgotten. Often it is this knowledge that helps one who is ill get through the day.

Fourth, never minimize the importance of hope. The story is told of a seriously ill man whose distraught wife went to the rebbe for advice on how to save her husband. "First," said the rebbe, "find the best doctor possible. Second, resort to prayer. Third, if these two fail, do not yet despair. Instead, hope for a miracle." Hope is always with us. Like a kaleidoscope, it may change from moment to moment, from wanting a complete cure, to a day without pain, to an end that is peaceful, but nevertheless hope endures as surely as spring follows winter and the rainbow follows a raging storm.

Finally, always be grateful to God for the miracles of medicine and the many opportunities we have to take better care of ourselves. My cancer was found at an early stage because I have been diligent about seeing my doctors regularly and having the appropriate tests from year to year. Remember the story about the man who found himself in the midst of a flood. The water began to rise, but he was reluctant to leave his home, and so he prayed: "God, please save me." A small boat came by and its passengers offered to take him to safety, but he said: "No. I am waiting for a sign from God," and he continued to pray. Then a helicopter flew by, and again he turned down this rescue attempt. In the meantime, the water got higher and higher until eventually he drowned. When he got to heaven, he approached God and started to complain: "God, I trusted You and prayed that You would save me. Why did You let me down?" and God replied: "You fool, I sent you a boat and a helicopter."

And so, it is with us. The fact that modern medicine continues to improve from month to month and year to year, that medical researchers continue to discover and develop new treatments and more precise testing, that doctors, nurses and caregivers share their wisdom and compassion with all of us—all these are gifts from God, reminders that although we cannot always control the final outcome, how we respond to life's challenges is well within our reach. If it is time for your mammogram or PSA test, your colonoscopy or next doctor's appointment, I urge you to take care of it now. Diligence may well save your life as it has saved mine time and time again.

I conclude now with some words of wisdom that came several months ago when I was asked to contribute to a book edited by Molly Meier called: *If I Only Had Five Things to Pass on From My Life They Would Be?* Here are my five:

Know Yourself: When I was in rabbinical school, I always assumed I would marry and have children. In fact, I said that in my synagogue there would be a nursery next to my study. After I was ordained and began serving God and the Jewish people, I discovered that I would never be able to have a career and a family and do both well. I stand in awe of those who can, but I know that I am not one of them. I chose to devote all my time and energy to my career, and I have never been sorry because I know that the people whose lives I touch are now part of my extended family.

Don't Worry: there are moments in every life when worry overwhelms us and inhibits our ability to function. For those times, I have developed my worry rule: sit down every morning for 10 minutes and worry as much as you want. Then get up, and welcome the many opportunities for growth and for good that each new day brings and make the most of them. There will be another 10 minutes tomorrow to worry again.

Always Try Your Best: Many people hesitate to try new things because they are afraid of failure. I believe the only true failure is in never daring to fail. Success feels good, but there is nothing wrong with failure, as long as we try our best and learn from our mistakes. The world moves forward every day because someone is willing to take the risk.

Live with Humility: Our sages taught: "People should have two pockets so they can reach into one or the other, according to their needs. In one pocket, there should be a slip of paper with the words 'For my sake was the world created' and in the other, the words 'I am but dust and ashes.'" In our day and age, humility seems to be a forgotten virtue. Being humble does not mean that we should deny or negate our achievements. On the contrary, taking pride in what we have accomplished brings great joy, but pausing to remember that we do not stand alone is even more enriching. Saying thank you on a regular basis to God who gives us the power to create, and to others who have helped us along the way, keeps us from becoming arrogant.

Maintain Your Sense of Humor: One way to deal with life's difficulties is by discovering and embracing the healing power of laughter. Many a tense moment has been relieved by bringing a bit of humor to the situation. An old Yiddish proverb advises: "Weep before God— laugh before people." Learning to laugh soothes the spirit, and learning to laugh at yourself keeps you from taking yourself too seriously. Laughter is contagious, and it makes the world a more pleasant place.

As I come now to the end of my remarks, and prepare to take your questions, I share with you my favorite poem, "The Road Not Taken" by Robert Frost, which pretty much sums up the way I feel about my life.

Two roads diverged in a yellow wood,
And sorry I could not travel both
And be on traveler, long I stood
And looked down one as far as I could

To where it bent in the undergrowth;
Then took the other, as just as fair
And having perhaps the better claim
Because it was grassy and wanted wear;

Though as for that, the passing there
Had worn them really about the same,
And both that morning equally lay
In leaves no step had trodden black.

Oh, I kept the first for another day!
Yet knowing how way leads on to way,
I doubted if I should ever come back.
I shall be telling this with a sigh

Somewhere ages and ages hence:
Two roads diverged in a wood, and I—
I took the one less traveled by,
And that has made all the difference. [5]

Agnes Baker Pilgrim (1924–)

"Thank you for water, the blood of Mother Earth."

At more than ninety years old, Agnes Baker Pilgrim is the senior
member of the Rogue River Band of Confederated Tribes of Siletz,
Oregon and chairs the International Council of Thirteen Indigenous
Grandmothers, a spiritual network of women elders representing
native peoples from all directions—north, south, east, and west. The
Grandmothers gather every six months in one another's communities
to pray, perform ancient rituals, educate, and persuade both world
leaders and everyday people to make peace and preserve the earth.
The Grandmothers' website notes that, "we [...] represent a global alliance of prayer, education, and healing for our Mother Earth, all Her
inhabitants, all the children, and the next seven generations to come." [6]

While they have many differences in their beliefs, customs, and
practices, the Grandmothers share common cause in serving as spiritual
and community leaders, sharing the wisdom of living in harmony with
the environment, as healers using natural medicines, and expressing
their grave concern about the state of the world. [7] The Grandmothers
travel the world, sharing their message of peace; they also actively use
Facebook, Twitter, and YouTube.

As one example of this spiritual and practical leadership, Baker Pilgrim, or "Mother Aggie," restored the Sacred Salmon Ceremony to the Rogue River Applegate region after 150 years of neglect. This ceremony reminds the people of the salmon's journey of life in the river and the sacred nature of the earth. More than a symbol, this ceremony is a call to action to wake up and get involved. In "Water," the speaker not only discusses her concern about pollution but also focuses on water's spiritual essence as "Mother Earth's blood," a gift from the Creator, one to be cherished and nurtured as part of humankind's caretaking responsibilities. [8] Pilgrim asserts, "We need to watch out for our animal kingdom that was created before us two-leggeds."

Baker Pilgrim speaks in many settings and places; this version is found as a general message on the internet to a broader audience. She calls on her listeners to recognize the gift of life, the rights of animals to exist and thrive, to be the "voice for the voiceless." Here she directly links spirituality and preservation with the sacred and interconnected nature of all living things.

After an introduction about herself and the Grandmothers, Baker Pilgrim directly moves into the urgency of water conservation. "Never in my life," she says, "did I think I would grow to this age and have to buy bottled water!" In plain language, she encourages her hearers to wake from their spiritual blindness and to preserve for the next seven generations of children. She counsels us to "try to do a better thing with our Mother Earth, for she sustains our lives."

* * *

"Water" (2005)[9]

2005

I'm Agnes Baker Pilgrim, a registered elder of the Confederated Tribes of Siletz Indians, and a granddaughter of Chief George Harney, the first elected chief of the Siletz Nation. I live in Grants Pass, Oregon. I came from a family of nine children. I was the third from the last child, born September 11, 1924, near headwaters of the Siletz River at Logsden,

Oregon. All of my siblings and parents are all gone, and it just leaves me now of my family.

I'm alumni of Southern Oregon University and a lifetime member of Amacron Delta Kappa. I have a bachelor's degree in psychology and a minor in Native American Studies, a culture instructor to my tribe, my other, Mother Earth, being a voice for the voices trying to prevent spiritual blindness.

On May 27, 2000, I was chosen by my tribe as a living legend and was honored along with other elders throughout the Northwest. I'm an elder mentor of Konaway Nika Tillicum at the Academy for Native American Youth, who live on campus at Southern Oregon University each year at the end of July.

October 19, 2002, I was a recipient of the Distinguished Alumni Award of the years 2002–2003, also was selected for an Imagine Award by Mediator Works, a Community Dispute Resolution Center of Medford, Oregon on March 9, 2003. October 11, 2004, at Phoenicia, New York, Thirteen International Indigenous Grandmothers formed an alliance, the first time in history. We gathered from the four directions in the land of the people of the Iroquois Confederacy, the Amazon Rain Forest, the Arctic Circle of North America, the Great Forest of the Amazon Northwest, the vast Plains of North America, the Highlands of Central America, the Black Hills of South Dakota, the mountains of Oaxaca, the desert of the American Southwest, and the mountains of Tibet and the Rain Forest of Central Africa. We joined with all those who honor the Creator and to all who work and pray for children, for world peace, and for the healing of our Mother Earth.

I've been traveling the world and I am very concerned about our water. Water is a very precious thing. It is, as native people call it, our Mother Earth's blood. Never in my life did I think I'd grow to this age and have to buy bottled water. To me it's frightening. I always tell people, "If you would jump in the bathtub and let me throw garbage in with you, you wouldn't like that."

So, I pray that this message will go to all people, to be able to teach their children and their children's children not to make a garbage dump out of rivers and streams. We need to start cleaning it up. Those swimmers in the water, they have the right to live just the same as anything else.

Without the animal kingdom we are gone, so we need to be the caretakers of our Mother Earth and to try to preserve the beautiful path that the Creator gave us to walk upon her. She sustains your life, and we need to reciprocate by doing a better thing and keeping the beauty that we have here today so that our seven generations ahead can be able to have what we have here now. We need to work diligently, as I say, I will continue to keep on keeping on until my heart is on the ground, to try to get people to hear, and to try to do a better thing with our Earth Mother, for she sustains our lives.

We need to be able to do all things. We need to be able to walk our path and be able to understand that this was a gift of our Creator to put us on this earth and to breathe into us, each breath, we need to give thanks for our lives. We need to watch out for our animal kingdom that was created before us two-leggeds, and we need to take care of them and be the voice for the voiceless, for they don't have a voice, as well as the green upon our Mother Earth. We need to be that voice.

We need to stop spiritual blindness. Our sacred grounds are being destroyed all over the continent. Because we don't have a steeple in a building called a church, they don't think these are spiritual places. We need to stop the spiritual blindness and to stand up and be that voice, and to try to preserve the things that the Mother Earth has left here for us, and to walk a better path.

I pray that those people out there will hear this message, and to be able to try to do a better way for our water, for our air, and try to bring back the cool burnings to our earth so that we won't have such awful hot fires anymore to clean off on the ground floor, and to put people hands-on back doing these kind of things. It would be a far better thing for us if we could band together and be able to preserve the beauty that we have here today.

Down here in southern Oregon, we have some plant life that grows nowhere else in the world and it needs to be preserved. We've already lost so much plant life that it's frightening. We need to try to preserve our seeds for the future generations ahead.

So, I want to thank all those that have these words to be able to understand we're all caretakers. We all need to join together for peace and to support and encourage one another, if we want to be able to stop and think about our women, our grandmothers, they are the natural nurturers of this earth.

And I'm very proud to be the chairman of the Thirteen Indigenous Grandmothers as we journey the world trying to preserve what we have here today and being that voice. I feel very honored to be able to be with the Thirteen Grandmothers from around the world to be able to get our heads of this country, to be able to tell nations all over that we have a right to gather the sacred medicines and end the violence against women and children.

They have the opportunity to meet the Dali Lama in October, but we don't have the funds. We want to be able to go to the pope to be able to get the pope [to say] in 1493 the Alexander VI was the one who started what happened to our people here all the many abuses. Many of them were killed off our tribes, [and] those tribes longer exist. I would like to be able to state that we need to stand together and go to see the pope, this new pope to see if cannot get him to revoke what happened, though he was not a part of that. Perhaps he would have heart enough to revoke what was done in 1493.

They came across the waters to destroy our people here because they weren't a religious people, they claimed. They were heathens and pagans and all these things, and they weren't a Christian is what they meant. It was all right to kill them off and take the land. And that's what started all this atrocities upon our people here, the First Nation people of the United States.

And, I pray that we get the funds to be able to take this message to the pope, and also to go to other countries to ask them to be able to pray for peace and to join us in that way. I know that we as Grandmothers have the wisdom and the knowledge to be able to be more firm and be able to make a voice throughout the countries for them to join us to preserve what we have, this beautiful earth, and to do a better thing with our water. Without the water, all things die. We need to keep the green so that we can have the fresh air that we so badly need. And I want to thank you for asking me to speak.

Notes

1 Paul Zakrzewski, "Pioneering Rabbi Who Softly Made Her Way," *The New York Times*, May 20, 2006, http://www.nytimes.com/2006/05/20/us/20religion.html

2 Elizabeth Blackwell (1821–1910) was the first woman to complete medical school in the United States.

3 Rabbi Sally J. Priesand, "Reflections on My Life as a Rabbi" (speech, Blackwell Award Ceremony, Hobart and William Smith Colleges, Geneva, NY, April 23, 2009), Hobart and William Smith Colleges, accessed March 1, 2018, http://www.hws.edu/news/transcripts/09blackwell_priesand.aspx

4 Pamela S. Nadell, *Women Who Would Be Rabbis: A History of Women's Ordination 1889–1985* (Boston, MA: Beacon Press, 1998).

5 As far as this author knows, this classic Robert Frost poem is in the public domain.

6 "Our Mission," International Council of Thirteen Indigenous Grandmothers, accessed November 28, 2017, http://www.grandmotherscouncil.org/our-mission

7 Paola Gianturco, *Grandmother Power: A Global Phenomenon* (Brooklyn, NY: Powerhouse Books, 2012), 175.

8 In my conversation with Mother Aggie, she told me how she thanks and blesses the water for nourishing her every time she takes a drink.

9 Agnes Baker Pilgrim, "Water" (speech, approx. 2005), Wisdom of the Elders, accessed March 1, 2018, http://www.wisdomoftheelders.org/turtle-island-storyteller-agnes-baker-pilgrim/Authenticity certified as this text was transcribed from the audio from YouTube.

Society

What is a woman's proper place in society? There are many competing narratives about this very question. Countries and cultures actively debate this question, and the answers, freedoms, and limits, are often influenced by religion. Controversies focus on who women are, their roles in society, the rights they have or are denied as citizens, and their rightful places in public and private life. Historically, religion can be an authority justifying a woman's limited role, and it can also become the foundation for finding new freedoms.

This section explores these themes in three speeches given in the United States more than a century apart. These orators all seek to define a woman's responsibilities within the larger cultural narrative context that men and women had separate spheres: men in the world and women at home. Is it the duty of women to stay at home, be wives and mothers, and to have their lives center around marriage, home, and hearth to take care of their men and raise moral children? Is it the duty of women to serve with the private "sphere" of the domestic life? Do wives and widows have rights to property, inheritance, voting, education, and legal status apart from their husbands? What civic responsibilities do women have to their nation? Are women human beings or simply the roles they play?

In the first speech, Clarina Howard Nichols brilliantly argues for women's equality because of their divinely appointed duties as wives and mothers. She expresses that women must have equality in property, ownership, and inheritance law to carry out their sanctioned responsibilities as women. Her rhetorical choices exhibit great wisdom as she both reinforces tradition with references to the Bible while indirectly making her arguments grounded within the parameters of this discourse community.

Phyllis Schlafly, in ironic contrast, argues against the Equal Rights Amendment in this second speech by attempting to preserve the "special privileges" of women as wives and mothers who would be harmed by consistent gender equality. She, too, refers to God as the author of gender roles which should be honored by preservation of male and female separation in law. Yet, Schlafly, like Howard, enshrines women's place as wives and mothers, and believes that too much equality may not be a good thing as women would lose their position in divorce law, exemption from the draft, and other privileges from being stay at home wives and mothers.

In the final speech of this section, famous feminist Elizabeth Cady Stanton argues that a woman's first duty is to herself, as a responsible individual and solitary soul, before any other role or responsibility can claim her. This address, given toward the end of her long career, speaks to the transcendent value of the individual soul as fully responsible and accountable for one's one life. For her, women's place in society is that of a fully human person and equal citizen.

Clarina Howard Nichols (1810–1885)

"Woman's responsibilities are equal to man's, I claim that God has endowed her with equal powers for their discharge."

Clarina Howard Nichols, like other more famous nineteenth-century women, actively engaged in the temperance and abolition movements. While not as celebrated as Elizabeth Cady Stanton and other early feminists, Nichols was a practical advocate for women's rights in the areas having the greatest impact in their lives: property ownership, inheritance, and guardianship of their children. Legally, a husband and wife were often considered to be a single person, with the husband taking charge of his wife's debts and property. Upon his death, she was entitled to one-third of the joint assets. This arrangement often impoverished widows and children. Nichols argued that women must be declared to have legal personhood to carry out "woman's responsibilities, and the means to fitly discharge them before Heaven."

As a child Nichols watched her father arbitrate debt cases and distribution of funds to the poor; she could see first-hand how the law discriminated against women and affected the real lives of families[1]

This experience and others fueled her passionate defense for women's rights under the law. This speech, delivered at the Woman's Rights Convention, Worcester, Massachusetts, in 1851, demonstrates Nichols' conviction, rhetorical skill and ability to read her audience well.

Nichols frames her call for equality in education and property rights as the necessary means to fulfilling "the responsibilities of a woman" to have the knowledge and financial resources to fulfill her role in the domestic sphere. Nichols uses biblical analogies, storytelling, and direct appeals to the fathers—or men—to assist and trust their wives with their property and livelihoods upon their deaths, so that their widows can carry out their roles as wives and mothers. By using many personal examples and positioning herself as "fulfilling every relation that is given a woman to fulfill," Nichols increases her ethos with her audience, from a woman demanding equal rights to a godly wife and mother seeking the legal means to fulfill their given roles. "For interests determine duties," she says, "and duties are the landmarks of spheres."

Just as Jesus Christ had a mission, argues Nichols, so does a woman have a mission as a mother to properly educate and take care of her children in the home. She proposes several times in the address that it is in the best interest of the man to help cultivate and encourage his wife's learning in practical life. "Yourselves must educate your wives in the conduct of your business. My friend, love is the best teacher in the world."

She even offers the idea that letting women own their own property will allow women to buy their husbands gifts and will help prevent divorces.

This speech is a rich example of effectively addressing to a potentially hostile audience by appealing to their personal benefit and values. She also encourages women to "cultivate their souls" through educating themselves "…to take life as we find it, and leave it better than we found it." Nichols did just that in her work for women's equality.

* * *

"The Responsibilities of a Woman" (1851)[2]

Second Annual Woman's Rights Convention

Worchester, New York

1851

My friends, I have made no preparation to address you. I left home, feeling that, if I had anything to do here, I should have the grace given me to do it; or if there should be any branch of the subject not sufficiently presented, I would present it. And now, friends, in following so many speakers, who have so well occupied the ground, I will come as a gleaner, and be as a Ruth among my fellow-laborers.

I commenced life with the most refined notions of woman's sphere. My pride of womanhood lay within this nice sphere. I know now how it was—perhaps because I am of mountain growth—but I could, even then, see over the barriers of that sphere, and see that, however easy it might be for me to keep within it, as a daughter, a great majority of women were outside its boundaries; driven thither by their own, or invited by the necessities and interests of those they loved. I saw our farmers' wives,—women esteemed for every womanly virtue,—impelled by emergencies, helping their husbands in labors excluded from the modern woman's sphere. I was witness, on one occasion, to a wife's helping her husband—who was ill and of feeble strength, and too poor to hire—to pile the logs, preparatory to clearing the ground that was to grow their daily bread; and my sympathies, which recognized in her act the self-sacrificing love of woman, forbade that I should judge her out of her sphere. For I felt in my heart that, if I were a wife and loved my husband, I, too, would help him when he needed help, even if it were to roll logs; and what true-hearted woman would not do the same?

But, friends, it is only since I have met the varied responsibilities of life, that I have comprehended woman's sphere; and I have come to regard it as lying within the whole circumference of humanity. If, as is claimed by the most ultra opponents of the wife's legal individuality, claimed as a conclusive, argument in favor of her legal nonentity, the interests of the parties are identical, then I claim, as a legitimate conclusion, that their spheres are also identical. For interests determine duties, and duties are the landmarks of spheres. Wherever a man may rightfully go, it is proper that woman should go, and share his responsibilities. Wherever my husband goes, thither would I follow him, if to the battle-field. No, I would not follow him there; I would hold him back by his coat-skirts, and say, "Husband, this is wrong. What will you gain by war? It will cost as much money to fight for a bag of gold, or a lot of land, as it will to pay the difference; and if you fight, our harvests are wasted, our hearths made desolate, our homes filled with sorrow, and vice and immorality roll back upon us from the fields of human slaughter." This is the way I would follow my husband where he cannot rightfully go. But I may not dwell longer on woman's sphere. I shall say very little of woman's rights; but I would lay the axe at the root of the tree. I would impress upon you woman's responsibilities, and the means fitly to discharge them before Heaven.

I stand before you, a mother, a sister, a daughter; filling every relation that it is given to woman to fill. And by the token that I have a husband, a father and brothers, whom I revere for their manliness, and love for their tenderness, I may speak to you with confidence, and say, I respect manhood. I love it when it aspires to the high destiny which God has opened to it. And it is because I have confidence in manhood, that I am here to press upon it the claims of womanhood. My first claim for woman is the means of education, that she may understand and be able to meet her responsibilities.

We are told very much of "Woman's Mission." Well, every mission supposes a missionary. Every missionary whom God sends out, every being who is called of God to labor in the vineyard of humanity, recognizes his call before the world does. Not the world—not even God's chosen people—recognized the mission of his Son, till he had proclaimed that mission, and sealed it with his dying testimony. And the world has not yet fully recognized the saving power of the mission of Jesus Christ. Now, if woman has a mission, she must first feel the struggle of the missionary in her own soul, and reveal it to her brother man, before the world will comprehend her claims, and accept her mission. Let her, then, say to man "Here, God has committed to me the little tender infant to be developed in body and mind to the maturity of manhood, womanhood, and I am ignorant of the means for accomplishing either. Give me knowledge, instruction, that I may develop its powers, prevent disease, and teach it the laws of its mental and physical organism." It is you, fathers, husbands, who are responsible for this instruction; your happiness is equally involved with ours. Yourselves must reap the harvest of our ignorance or knowledge. If we suffer, you suffer also; both must suffer or rejoice in our mutual offspring.

I have introduced this subject of woman's responsibilities, that I might, if possible, impress upon you a conviction of the expediency and duty of yielding our right to the means that will enable us to be the helpers of men, in the true sense of helpers. A gentleman said to me, not long since, "I like your woman's rights, since I find it is the right of women to be good for something and help their husbands." Now, I do not understand the term helpmeet, as applied to woman, to imply all that has come to be regarded as within its signification. I do not understand that we are at liberty to help men to the devil. I believe it is our mission to help them heavenward, to the full development and right enjoyment of their being. I would say, in reference to the rights of woman, it has come to be forgotten that, as the mother of the race, her rights are the rights of men also, the rights of her sons. As a mother, I may speak to you, freeman, fathers, of the rights of my sons—of every mother's sons—to the most perfect and vigorous development of their energies which the mother can secure to them by the application and through the use of all her God-given powers of body or of mind. It is in behalf of our sons, the future men of the republic, as well as for our daughters, its future mothers, that we claim the full development of our energies by education, and legal protection in the control of all the issues and profits of ourselves, called property.

As a parent, I have educated myself with reference to the wants of my children, that if, by the bereavements of life, I am left their sole parent, I can train them to be good and useful citizens. Such bereavement has left me the sole parent of sons by a first marriage. And how do the laws of the state protect the right of these sons to their mother's fostering care? The laws say that, having married again, I am a legal nonentity and cannot "give bonds" for the faithful discharge of my maternal duties; therefore, I shall not be their guardian. Having, in the first instance, robbed me of the property qualification for giving bonds, alienating my right to the control of my own earnings, the state makes its own injustice the ground for defrauding myself and children of the mutual benefits of our God-ordained relations; and others, destitute of every qualification and motive which my mother's love insures to them, may "give bonds" and become the legal guardians of my children!

I address myself to you, fathers, I appeal to every man who has lived a half-century, if the mother is not the most faithful guardian of her children's interests? If you were going on a long journey, to be absent for years, in the prosecution of business, or in the army or navy, would you exclude your wives from the care and guardianship of your children? Would you place them and the means for their support in any other hands than the mother's? If you would, you have married beneath yourselves. Then I ask you how it happens that, when you die, your estates are cut up, and your children, and the means for their support, consigned to others' guardianship, by laws which yourselves have made or sworn to defend? Do you reply that women are not qualified by education for the business transactions involved in such guardianship? It is for this I ask that they may be educated. Yourselves must educate your wives in the conduct of your business.

My friends, love is the best teacher in the world. Fathers, husbands, you do not know how fast you can teach, nor what apt scholars you will find in your wives and daughters, if, with loving confidence, you call them to your aid, and teach them those things in which they can aid you, and acquire the knowledge, which is "power," to benefit those they love. Would it not soothe your sick bed, would it not pluck thorns from your dying pillow, to confide in your wife that she could conduct the business on which your family relies for support, and, in case of your death, keep your children together, and educate them to go out into the world with habits of self-reliance and self-dependence? And do you know that, in withholding from your companions the knowledge and inducements which would fit them thus to share your cares, and relieve you in the emergencies of business, you deny them the richest rewards of affection? for "it is more blessed to give than to receive" [Acts 20:35]. Do you know that they would only cling the closer to you in the stern conflicts of life, if they were thus taught that you do not undervalue their devotion and despise their ability? Call woman to your side in the loving confidence of equal interests and equal responsibilities, and she will never fail you.

But I would return to woman's responsibilities, and the laws that alienate her means to discharge them. And here let me call your attention to my position, that the law which alienates the wife's right to the control of her own property, her own earnings lies at the foundation of all her social and legal wrongs. I have already shown you how the alienation of this right defrauds her of the legal guardianship of her children, in case of the father's death. I need not tell you, who see it every day in the wretched family of the drunkard, that it defrauds her of the means of discharging her responsibilities to her children and to society during the husband's life, when he proves recreant to his obligations, and consumes her earnings in the indulgence of idle and sinful habits. I know it is claimed by many, as a reason why this law should not be disturbed, that it is only the wives of reckless and improvident husbands who suffer under it operation.

But, friends, I stand here prepared to show that, as an unjust law of general application, it is even more fruitful of suffering to the wives of what are called good husbands,—husbands who love and honor their wives while living, but, dying, leave them and their maternal sympathies to the dissecting-knife of the law. I refer you to the legal-provision for the widow. The law gives her the use only of one-third of the estate which they have accumulated by their joint industry. I speak of the real estate; for, in the majority of estates, the personal property is expended in paying the debts and meeting the expenses of settlement.

Now, I appeal to any man here, whose estate is sufficient to support either or both in comfort, and give them Christian burial, and yet is so limited that the use of one-third of it will support neither, whether his wife's interests are equally protected with his own, by the laws which "settle" his estate in the event of his dying first. Let me tell you a story to illustrate the "support" which, it is claimed, compensates the wife for the alienation of her earnings to the control of the husband. In my native town lived a single sister, of middle age. She had accumulated something, for she was capable in all the handicrafts pursued by women of her class. She married a worthy man, poor in this world's goods, and whose children were all settled in homes of their own. She applied her means, and, by the persevering use of her faculties, they secured a snug home, valued at some five hundred dollars, he doing what his feeble health permitted towards the common interest. In the course of years, he died, and two-thirds of that estate was divided among his grown children; one-third remaining to her. No, she could only have the use of one-third, and must keep it in good repair,—the law said so! The use of less than two hundred dollars in a homestead, on condition of "keeping it in good repair," was the legal pittance of this poor woman, to whom, with the infirmities of age, had come the desolation of utter bereavement! The old lady patched and toiled, beautiful in her scrupulous cleanliness. The neighbors remembered her, and many a choice bit found its way to her table. At length she was found in her bed paralyzed; and never, to the day of her death,—three years,—could she lift her hand or make known the simplest want of her nature; and yet her countenance was agonized with the appeals of a clear and sound intellect.

And now, friends, how did the laws support and protect this poor widow? I will tell you. They set her up at auction, and struck her off to the man who had a heart to keep her at the cheapest rate! Three years she enjoyed the pauper's support, then died; and when the decent forms of a pauper's burial were over, that third was divided—as had been the other two-thirds—among her husband's "well-to-do" children. And is it for such protection that the love of fathers, brothers, husbands, "represents" woman in the legislative halls of the freest people on earth? O, release to us our own, that we may protect ourselves, and we will bless you! If this old lady had died first, the laws would have protected her husband in appropriating the entire estate to his comfort or his pleasure! I asked a man, learned and experienced in jurisprudence by a half-century's discharge of the duties of legislator, administrator, guardian and probate judge, why the widow is denied absolute control of her third, there being no danger of creating "separate interests" when the husband is in his grave. He replied that it was to prevent a second husband from obtaining possession of the property of a first, to the defrauding of his children, which would be the result if the widow married again. Here, the law giving the control of the wife's earnings to the husband is made legal reason for cutting her off at his death with a pittance, so paltry, that, if too infirm to eke out a support by labor, she becomes a pauper! For if the law did not give the wife's earnings to the control and possession of a first husband, it would have no such excuse for excluding the second husband, or for defrauding herself, and her children by a subsequent marriage, of her earnings in the estate of the first husband. But having legalized the husband's claim to the wife's earnings, by a law of universal application, our legislators have come to legislate for widows on the ground that they have no property rights in the estates which have swallowed up their entire earnings! They have come to give the preference of rights to the children of the husband; and sons, as well as daughters, are defrauded, legislated out of their interests in their mother's property. For, the estate not being divided, when the wife dies, the earnings of a first wife are divided among the children of a second wife, to the prejudice of the children of the first wife.

We ask for equal property rights, by the repeal of the laws which divert the earnings of the wife from herself and her heirs.

O men! in the enjoyment of well-secured property rights, you beautify your snug homesteads, and say within your hearts, "Here I may sit under my own vine and fig-tree; here have I made the home of my old age." And it never occurs to you that no such blissful feeling of security finds rest in the bosom of your wives. The wife of a small householder reflects that if her husband should be taken from her by death, that home must be divided, and a corner in the kitchen, a corner in the garret, and a "privilege" in the cellar, be set off to her use, and she called, in legal phrase, an "incumbrance"! Or if she chooses the alternative of renting her fractional accommodations, and removing to other quarters, her sweet home-associations—all that is left of her wedded love—are riven. The fireside that had been hallowed by family endearments, the chair vacant to other eyes, but to hers occupied by the loved husband still, all are desecrated by the law that drives her from the home which she had toiled and sacrificed to win for herself and loved ones, and she goes out to die under a vine and a fig-tree strange to her affections; and, it may be, as in the case before mentioned, to find them wither away like Jonah's gourd, in absolute pauperism!

But I will tell you a story illustrating how women view these things. It is not long since a gentleman of my acquaintance, who had often been heard give his wife credit for having contributed equally to his success in laying up a property, was admonished by disease of the propriety of making a "will." He called his wife to him, and addressed her thus: "My dear, I have been thinking that the care of a third of my estate will be a burden to you, and that it will be better for you to have an annuity equal to your personal wants, and divide the rest among the children. The boys will supply you, if you should, from any unforeseen circumstance, need more. You can trust our boys to do what is right." "O yes, my dear," replied the wife, "we have excellent boys. You entrust to them the care of your business; and I could let them act as my agents in the care of my thirds. And I think, husband, that will be better. For there is this to be considered: We have other children, and differences obtain in their circumstances. You have seen these things, and, when one and another needed, you have opened your purse and given them help. When you are gone, there may still occur these opportunities for aiding them, and I should be glad to have it in my power to do as you have done. Besides, I have sometimes thought you had not done so well by the girls; and it would be very grateful to my feelings to make up the difference from my share of what our mutual efforts have accumulated."

Now, brothers, I appeal to you, whether you do not as much enjoy conferring benefits as receiving them? You have a wife whom you love. You present her with a dress, perhaps. And how rich you feel, that your love can give gifts! Women like to receive presents of dresses; I enjoy to have my husband give me dresses. And women like to give presents to their husbands—a pair of slippers, or something of that sort. But they have no money of their own, and their thought is, "If I give my husband this, he will say to himself, It's of no account; it all comes out of my pocket in the end!" That is the feeling which rankles in the hearts of wives, whose provident husbands do not dream that they are not better content with gifts than their rights. We like, all of us, to give good gifts to those we love; but we do not want our husbands to give us something to give back to them. We wish to feel, and have them feel, that our own good right hands have won for them the gift prompted by our affection; and that we are conferring, from our own resources, the same pleasure and happiness which they confer on us by benefits given. (Great cheering.)

But I had not exhausted the wrongs growing out of this alienation of the wife's right to her earnings. There is a law in Vermont—and I think it obtains in its leading features in most, if not all, the states of the Union—giving to the widow, whose husband dies childless (she may or may not be the mother of children by a former marriage), a certain portion of the estate, and the remaining portion to his heirs. Till the autumn of 1850, a Vermont widow, in such cases, had only one-half the estate, however small; the other half was set off to her husband's heirs, if he had any; but, if he had none, the state put it in its own treasury, leaving the widow to a pauper's fate, unless her own energies could eke out a living by economy and hard toil! A worthy woman in the circle of my acquaintance, whose property at marriage paid for a homestead worth five hundred dollars, saw this law divide a half of it to the brothers and sisters of her husband at his death, and herself is left, in her old age, to subsist on the remaining half! In 1850, this law was so amended that the widow can have the whole property, if it be not more than one thousand dollars, and the half of any sum over than amount; the other half going to the husband's family; or, if he happen not to leave any fiftieth cousin Tom, Dick or Harry, in the old World or the New, she may have it all! Our legislators tell us it is right to give the legal control of our earnings to the husband, because "in law" he is held responsible for our support, and is obliged to pay our debts (?), and must have our earnings to do it with! Ah, I answer, but why don't the state give us some security, then, for support during our life; or if it loses the husband from all obligation to see that we are supported after he is in his grave, why, like a just and shrewd business agent, does it not release to us the "consideration" of that support—our earnings in the property which he leaves at his death?

The law taking from the wife the control of her earnings is a fruitful source of divorces. To regain control of her earnings for the support of her children, many a woman feels compelled to sue for a divorce. I am here in the hope that I can say something for the benefit of those who must suffer, because they cannot speak and show that they have wrongs to be redressed. It would ill become us, who are protected by love, or shielded by circumstances, to hold our peace while our sisters and their dependent children are mutilated in their hopes and their entire powers of existence, by wrongs against which we can protest till the legislators of the land shall hear and heed.

I was speaking of woman's self-created resources as necessary means for the discharge of her duties. Created free agents that we might render to God an acceptable and voluntary service, our Maker holds each human being accountable for the discharge of individual, personal responsibilities. Man, under his present disabilities, cannot come up to the full measure of his own responsibilities; much less can he discharge his own and woman's too. Hence, in taking from woman any of the means which God has given her ability to acquire, he takes from her the means which God has given her for the discharge of her own duties, and thereby adds to the burthen (sic) of his own undischarged responsibilities. In taking from us our means of self-development, men expect us to discharge our duties even as the Jews were expected to make brick without straw. If we are not fitted to be capable wives and mothers,—as contended by a gentleman on the stand yesterday,—if we make poor brick, it is because our brother man has stolen our straw. Give us back our straw, brothers,—there is plenty of it,—and we will make you good brick. Brick we must make—men say so; then give us our straw,—we cannot take it. We are suffering; the race is suffering from the ill-performance of our duties. We claim that man has proved himself incompetent to be the judge of our needs. His laws concerning our interests show that his intelligence fails to prescribe means and conditions for the discharge of our duties. We are the best judges of the duties, as well as the qualifications, appropriate to our own department of labor; and should hold in our own hands, in our own right, means for acquiring the one and comprehending the other.

I have spoken of woman's legal disabilities as wife and mother; and adverted to the law which diverts from the wife the control of her own earnings, as a fruitful source of divorces. Increasing facilities for divorce are regarded by a majority of Christian men as significant of increasing immorality, and tending to weaken the sanctity of the marriage relation. But an examination of legislative proceedings will show that sympathy for suffering woman is the real source of these increasing facilities; and I am frank to say, that I consider man's growing consciousness of the wrongs to which wives and their helpless children are subject, by the laws which put it in the power of the husband and father to wrest from them the very necessaries of life, consuming their sole means of support,—the earnings of the mother,—as heralding a good time coming, when every woman, as well as every man, "may sit under her own vine" [Micah 4:4].

Let me illustrate by relating one, among many incidents of the kind, which have fallen under my observation. In travelling, some eighteen years ago, across the Green Mountains from Albany, a gentleman requested my interest in behalf of a young woman, whose history he gave me before placing her under my care, as a fellow-passenger. Said he, She was born here; is an orphan, and the mother of two young children, with no means of support but her earnings. She was a capable girl, and has been an irreproachable wife. From a love of the social glass, her husband in a few years became a drunkard and a brute; neglected his business, and expended their entire living. She struggled bravely, but in vain. At length, just before the birth of her youngest child! he pawned the clothing which she had provided for herself and babes, sold her only bed, and drove her into the streets to seek from charity aid in her hour of trial. After her recovery, she went to service, keeping her children with her. But he pursued her from place to place annoying her employers, collecting her wages by process of law, and taking possession of every garment not on her own or children's persons. Under these circumstances, and by the help of friends who pitied her sorrows, she, with her hatless and shoeless children, was flying from their "legal protector," half clothed, to New Hampshire, where friends were waiting to give her employment in a factory, till a year's residence should enable her to procure a divorce! Now, friends, if under New York laws this poor woman had enjoyed legal control of her own earnings, she might have retained her first home, supported her children, and, happy as a mother, endured hopefully the burden of unrequited affection, instead of flying to New Hampshire to regain possession of her alienated property rights, by the aid of "divorce facilities."

But, alas! not yet have I exhausted that fountain of wrongs growing out of the alienation of the wife's property rights. It gives to children criminals for guardians, at the same time that it severs what God hath joined together—the mother and her child! By the laws of all these United States, the father is in all cases the legal guardian of the child, in preference to the mother; hence, in cases of divorce for the criminal conduct of the father, the children are confided, by the natural operation of the laws, to the guardianship of the criminal party. I have a friend who, not long since, procured a divorce from her husband,—a libertine and a drunkard,—and by the power of law he wrested from her their only child, a son of tender age. Think of this, fathers, mothers! It is a sad thing to sever the marriage relation when it has become a curse—a demoralizing (?) thing; but what is it to sever the relation between mother and child, when that relation is a blessing to both, and to society? What is it to commit the tender boy to the training of a drunken and licentious father? The state appoints guardians for children physically orphaned; and much more should it appoint guardians for children morally orphaned. When it uses its power to imprison and hang the man, it is surely responsible for the moral training of the boy! But to return. I have asked learned judges why the state decrees that the father should retain the children, thus throwing upon the innocent mother the penalty which should fall upon the guilty party only? Say they, "It is because the father has the property; it would not be just (?) to burden the mother with the support of his children." O justice, how art thou perverted! Here again, is the unrighteous alienation of the wife's earnings made the reason for robbing the suffering mother of all that is left to her of a miserable marriage—her children! I appeal to Christian men and women, who would preserve the marriage relation inviolate, by discouraging increased divorce facilities, if prevention of the necessity be not the better and more hopeful course,—prevention by releasing to the wife means for the independent discharge of her duties as a mother. And I appeal to all present, whether, sacred as they hold the marriage relation, Christian men have not proved to the world that there is a something regarded by them as even more sacred—the loaf! The most scrupulous piety cites Bible authority for severing the marriage tie; but when has piety or benevolence put forth its hand to divide to helpless and dependent woman an equal share of the estate which she has toiled for, suffered for, in behalf of her babes, as she would never have done for herself—only to be robbed of both?

If the ground of the divorce be the husband's infidelity, the law allows him to retain the children and whole estate; it being left with the court to divide to the wife (in answer to her prayer to that effect) a pittance called alimony, to keep starvation at bay. If the babe at her breast is decreed to her from its helplessness, it is, at her request, formally laid before the court; and the court has no power even to decree a corresponding pittance for its support. The law leaves her one hope of bread for her old age which should not be forgotten—if he dies first, she is entitled to dower! But let the wife's infidelity be the ground of divorce, and the laws send her Out into the world, childless, without alimony, and cut off from her right of dower; and property which came by her remains his forever! What a contrast! He, the brutal husband, sits in the criminal's bench to draw a premium, be rid of an incumbrance; for what cares he for the severing of a tie that had ceased to bind him to his wife, that perhaps divided between him and a more coveted companion! If we are the weaker sex, O, give us equal protection with the stronger sex!

Now, my friends, you will bear me witness that I have said nothing about woman's right to vote or make laws. I have great respect for manhood. I wish to be able to continue to respect it. And when I listen to Fourth-of-July orations and the loud cannon, and reflect that these are tributes of admiration paid to our fathers because they compelled freedom for themselves and sons from the hand of oppression and power, I look forward with greater admiration on their sons who, in the good time coming will have won for themselves the unappropriated glory of having given justice to the physically weak; to those who could not, if they would, and would not, if they could, compel it from the hands of fathers, brothers, husbands and sons! I labor in hope; for I have faith that when men come to value their own rights, as means of human happiness, rather than of paltry gain, they will feel themselves more honored in releasing than in retaining the "inalienable rights" of woman.

Brothers, you ask us to accept the protection of your LOVE, and the law says that is sufficient for us, whether it feeds or robs us of our bread. You admit that woman exceeds man in self-sacrificing love; her devotion to you has passed into a proverb. Yet, for all this, you refuse to intrust your interests to her love. You do not feel safe in your interests without the protection of equal laws. You refuse to trust even the mother's love with the interests of her children! How, then, do you ask of us—you, who will not trust your interests to the love of a mother, wife, daughter, or sister—why do you ask of us to dispense with the protection of equal laws, and accept instead the protection of man's affection?

I would offer, in conclusion, a few thoughts on education. I would say to my sisters, lest they be discouraged under existing disabilities from attempting it,—we can educate ourselves. It may be that you hesitate, from a supposed inferiority of intellect. Now, I have never troubled myself to establish woman's intellectual equality. The inequality of educational facilities forbids us to sustain such a position by facts. But I have long since disposed of this question to my own satisfaction, and perhaps my conclusion will inspire you with confidence to attempt equal—I would hope superior—attainments, for man falls short of the intelligence within reach of his powers. We all believe that the Creator is both omniscient and omnipotent, wise and able to adapt means to the ends he had in view. We hold ourselves created to sustain certain relations as intelligent beings, and that God has endowed us with capabilities equal to the discharge of the duties involved in these relations.

Now, let us survey woman's responsibilities within the narrowest sphere to which any common-sense man would limit her offices. As a mother, her powers mould and develop humanity, intellectual, moral and physical. Next to God woman is the creator of the race as it is and as it shall be. I ask, then, Has God created woman man's inferior? If so, he has been false to his wisdom, false to his power, in creating an inferior being for superior work! But if it be true, as all admit, that woman's responsibilities are equal to man's, I claim that God has endowed her with equal powers for their discharge.

And how shall we develop these powers? My sisters, for your encouragement, I will refer to my own experience in this matter. I claim to be self-educated. Beyond a single year's instruction in a high school for young men and women, I have enjoyed no public educational facilities but the common school which our Green Mountain state opens to all her sons and daughters. Prevented by circumstances from availing myself of the discipline of a classical school of the highest order, and nerved by faith in my ability to achieve equal attainments with my brother man, I resorted to books and the study of human nature, with direct reference to the practical application of my influence and my acquirements to my woman's work,—the development of the immortal spirit for the accomplishment of human destiny.

And my own experience is, that the world in which we live and act, and by which we are impressed, is the best school for woman as well as man. Practical life furnishes the best discipline for our powers. It qualifies us to take life as we find it, and leave it better than we found it. I have been accustomed to look within my own heart to learn the springs of human action. By it I have read woman, read man; and the result has been a fixed resolution, an indomitable courage to do with my might what my hands find to do for God and humanity. And in doing, I have best learned my ability to accomplish, my capacity to enjoy. In the light of experience, I would say to you, my sisters, the first thing is to apply ourselves to the intelligent discharge of present duties, diligently searching out and applying all knowledge that will qualify us for higher and extended usefulness. Be always learners, and don't forget to teach. As individuals, as mothers, we must first achieve a knowledge of the laws of our physical and mental organisms; for these are the material which we work upon and the instruments by which we work; and, to do our work well, we must understand and be able to apply both. Then we need to understand the tenure of our domestic and social relations,—the laws by which we are linked to our kind. But I cannot leave this subject without briefly calling your attention to another phase of education.

Early in life, my attention was called to examine the value of beauty and accomplishments as permanent grounds of affection. I could not believe that God had created so many homely women, and suffered all to lose their beauty in the very maturity of their powers, and yet made it our duty to spend our best efforts in trying to look pretty. We all desire to be loved; and can it be that we have no more lasting claims to admiration than that beauty and those accomplishments which serve us only in the spring-time of life? Surely our days of dancing and musical performance are soon over, when musical instruments of sweeter tone cry "Mother." (Loud cheers.)

What, then, shall we do for admiration when stricken in years? Has not God endowed us with some lasting hold upon the affections? My sister, I can only find lasting charms in that thorough culture of the mind and heart which will enable us to win upon man's higher and better nature. If you have beauty and accomplishments, these address themselves to man's lower nature—his passions; and when age has robbed you of the one, and him of the other, you are left unloved and unlovely! Cultivate, then, your powers of mind and heart, that you may become necessary to his better and undying sympathies. Aid him in all the earnest work of life; and secure his aid in your self-development for noble purposes, by impressing upon him that you are in earnest. Sell your jewelry, if need be, abate your expenditures for show; and appropriate your means, and time spent in idle visiting, to the culture of your souls. Then will his soul respond to your worth, and the ties that bind you endure through time, and make your companions in eternity!

Let the daughters be trained for their responsibilities; and though you may say, "We do not know whom they will marry, whether a lawyer, a doctor, or farmer," if you educate them for practical life, by giving them general useful knowledge, their husbands can teach them the details of their mutual business interests, as easily as the new responsibilities of maternity will teach them the ways and means of being qualified to discharge its duties.

Educate your daughters for practical life, and you have endowed them better than if you had given them fortunes. When a young girl of fourteen, I said to my father, Give me education, instead of a setting out in the world, if you can give me but one. If I marry, and am poor in this world's goods, I can educate my children myself. If my husband should be unfortunate, the sheriff can take his goods; but no creditor can attach the capital invested here. (Touching her forehead.) (Loud cheers.) And my education has not been only bread, but an inexhaustible fund of enjoyment, in all the past of my life.

Phyllis Schlafly (1924–2016)

The Positive Woman opposes ERA because she knows it would be harmful to women, to men, to children, to the family, to local self-government, and to society as a whole.[3]

By any measure, controversial and conservative leader Phyllis Schlafly was a force of nature. Her career as an activist included speaking and writing against abortion, same-sex marriage, and other feminist issues.

She campaigned most passionately against the Equal Rights Amendment to the U.S. Constitution which proposed removing any reference to sex and gender in state and federal laws.

Raised Roman Catholic, Schlafly was a mother of six children, writer, speaker, lawyer activist, and founder of the Eagle Forum. Schlafly galvanized conservatives all over the United States during the 1970s to STOP (Stop Taking Our Privileges) ERA. She wrote or edited more than 20 books, made frequent appearances on national media, and campaigned tirelessly in state legislatures all over the country against ratification of the Equal Rights Amendment. Feminist Betty Friedan reportedly said that Schlafly should be burned at the stake like a religious heretic for her ardent opposition to ERA.

This address, given January 1, 1975, in St. Paul, Minnesota, is typical of her plain-spoken, extemporaneous style. Her commitment to traditional "Judeo-Christian values" influenced politicians to reject the ERA. The opening quotation conveys a summary of her views: the positive woman "knows God made her...why she's here, and she has her scale of values in order."[4] She argued that women in the United States enjoy special privileges as wives and mothers as men, by law, had to support their families in marriage and through alimony upon divorce.

Following her line of reasoning, Schlafly establishes an "us and them" dichotomy between herself, representing traditional wives and mothers, and the "women's libbers." From this position, she states the arguments of the "proponents" that women are unequal and then argues against each. She names existing laws providing protection for equal pay and education, and then offers names and examples of what the law can mean. Perhaps Schlafly's most influential claim against the ERA was that daughters and mothers would have to register for the draft and be sent to war. She also argued that other societal losses would result from a ratified ERA: the end of single-sex colleges, male and female students on the same athletic teams, the same physical standards for men and women who work "in the manual labor theater," and more power to the federal government.

Between 1972 and 1982, the ERA failed ratification after a turbulent decade of debating state to state and in the media. Schlafly and her social movement succeeded in influencing the states and the public that the ERA was too much for a nation growing more conservative in the 1980s.

* * *

"The Equal Rights Amendment (ERA)" (1975)[5]

St. Paul, Minnesota

January 1, 1975

There are two contrary views of women in our society today. One is, I think, best demonstrated by an old story that goes like this: They say when men die and go to heaven, they are required to go through one of two doors. On the first door are inscribed the words "Men Who Are Dominated by Their Wives." Over the other door, there's "Men Who Dominate Their Wives." And there is always as very long line in front of the first door, and hardly ever any line in front of the second door. But one day, an insignificant-looking man turned up in front of the door that said, "Men Who Dominate Their Wives." And one of his friends called over from the second line and said, "Say, Harry, what are you doing standing in front of that door?" And Harry replied, "My wife told me I had to stand in front of that door."

This demonstrates one view of women. There's another view of women which is popularized by the Women's Liberation Movement, and which was most succinctly stated in a commercial which was developed by the National Organization for Women, the principal women's lib group. And it was one of the television spots in many areas, also in newspapers and magazines and services. This commercial shows the picture of a darling, curly-headed child, and the caption over the picture is, "This normal, healthy child was born with a handicap: it was born female." Now that is the starting assumption of the Women's Lib Movement, that somebody—it isn't clear who; maybe God, maybe the establishment, or society, or a conspiracy of male chauvinist pigs—have dealt women a foul blow by making us female, and it is up to legislation or our constitutional amendments to remedy this terrible injustice. And that has been a frame of reference in the way they start.

And so, they proposed the Equal Rights Amendment to the Constitution as this remedy for centuries of injustice to women. The proponents of the Equal Rights Amendment go around the country giving us a tiresome litany of past injustices that this world can remedy. They cry out about women not having the right to vote, and women not being able to serve on a jury, and women not being able to go to law school or medical school, and other obsolete things that have long since passed in our society. I really think you have to have psychological problems or have a chip on your shoulder because of what time in this country women have had the right to vote; it's been more than fifty years since this problem was solved. I think the Equal Rights Amendment was very well summed up at the Virginia legislative hearing, by a woman who identified herself as ninety-three years old and a suffragette who had been campaigning for women's rights for more than half a century. She said the proponents of the Equal Rights Amendment are fifty years behind the times; they are fighting a battle that has been long since won. And I think she said it very well, because all these things that they've criticized have long since been passed in our society. Yet they keep talking about it and crying about it. They simply are not relevant to the world that we live in today.

I debated one Ph.D. from the University of Wisconsin who started her talk by saying, "Our sisters in other lands have made more progress towards women's rights than we have in the United States." I said, "Please name one other country where women are as well off as they are in the United States." And she had no reply. And yet, supporters of the Equal Rights Amendment go about saying, "Women in this country are kept in serfdom. They are treated like cattle. They are second-class citizens. They are statistically a non-person." This simply isn't true, and those are not exaggerated statements; those are all actual quotes from proponents of the Equal Rights Amendment.

Now, if you were to attend the state legislation hearings around the country (as I have been to a number of them), the first thing that will strike you when you listen to the arguments of the proponents is that they have no case. They are not able to cite any injustices against women that ERA will remedy; they are not able to cite any laws discriminating against women that ERA will wipe out; they are not able to cite any rights or benefits that ERA will give them. Many people who have supported the Equal Rights Amendment in good faith have done so because somehow they identify it with the slogan "equal pay for equal work." Now, that's a good objective anybody would support; I did not encounter one person who was against equal pay for equal work. But the thing you find out when you listen to the lawyers for the proponents is that ERA has absolutely nothing to do with equal pay for equal work. As a matter of fact, there is absolutely no way that the Equal Rights Amendment will benefit women in the area of employment. As a matter of fact, when I made that last statement in a debate with Congresswoman Martha Griffiths, who is the leading congressional proponent, she replied, "I never claimed it would."

Now they've closed their case, because most people who have supported ERA have done so because they thought it would benefit women in the area where everyone knows there has been discrimination in the past. But it will not, and every lawyer who has appeared at the state legislative hearings has admitted that ERA will not benefit women at all in the business of employment. ERA doesn't apply to private industry; it only applies to federal and state laws. And the second reason is that there's no way it can consider the effect of the Equal Employment Opportunity Act of 1972. Although this is very specific, it applies to power and fame and emotion. It sets up the enforcing mechanism, the agency that handles the complaints. If any woman thinks she has been discriminated against, she can file her claim; it won't cost her any money; she won't have to hire a lawyer.

When the women won a $30 million settlement against U.S. Steel, the company was mandated to hire twenty percent women in its production. Now, you may or may not think that hiring women in production in steel mills is an advance in the cause of women but, at any event, those jobs are there if she wants them. And the Equal Rights Amendment will add absolutely nothing to it. And it is a measure of the hypocrisy and the fraud of the Equal Rights Amendment that proponents continue to go about speaking to uninformed groups, and the way they have garbled the law and identify ERA with equal pay for equal work, while their lawyers are supposed to admit and do admit at the state legislative hearings that ERA will do absolutely nothing for women in that area.

Now let's take the matter of education. ERA will do nothing whatever for women in the field of education but the fact of the Education Amendments of 1972. Here again we have a very old law. It applies to different parts of magnet schools, any school that has any federal aid whatsoever covering additions, hiring, promotions, scholarships, grants of all kinds. Well, there's no way that ERA could add anything to women's opportunity to get an education. Now there is an exception to the education amendments of 1972; they exempted admissions to single-sex colleges if they have been traditionally single-sex for many years. Now, there were a number of colleges that actually preferred to retain their single-sex status. We could name a few—Smith, Wellesley, Bryn Mawr, Mount Holyoke—a bunch of exemptions that, of course, would not be constitutional if ERA were ratified. It can exempt any present aid or scholarship grant of any kind whatsoever. And this, of course, would apply to possibly ninety percent of the colleges. You see, a single-sex college by definition discriminates on the basis of sex: a girls' college discriminates against boys, and a boys' college discriminates against girls. Now, what the ERA proponent lawyers will tell you, ERA will end single-sex colleges, and they want it to. They do not feel that one should have the right to make a single-sex college that would discriminate on the basis of sex. Now, I know that most of the people of our day seem to prefer co-ed colleges. I don't see how this advances the cause for anybody to deny those who prefer single-sex colleges their right to attend. But that is the understandable result of ERA that cannot be disputed.

Now, when Congress passed the Education Amendments of 1972, it fell to the Department of Health, Education and Welfare for implementation, and it took HEW two years to produce their regulations to implement it.

And so in June 1974, HEW came out with eighty pages of regulations. And there was quite an explosion when they came out, because these regulations said that all sex education classes had to be co-ed, that all gym classes had to be co-ed, and that fraternities and sororities could not continue to operate as single-sex organizations on the campus of any college that received any general revenue. Well, there was quite an explosion, and Jasper Weinberger held a press conference within a week, and said, "I can't exempt the rest of us without specific authority from Congress because I believe that the law requires us to make all these things co-ed."

So then, the Congressmen began to hear from the fraternities and sororities and gym directors that they began to impact through HEW regulations. And then the proponents of the Education Amendments of 1972 threw up their hands and said, "Oh, we didn't mean this when we passed that law!" But, HEW thought it did. So, the Congressmen proposed a draft of a rather quickie amendment, and they got it through both houses in record speed; it passed just before Christmas, and it specifically exempted from the Education Amendments of 1972 as related to HEW regulations: gym classes, fraternities, sororities, Girl Scouts, Boys Scouts, YWCA, YMCA, boys' clubs, and girls' clubs. And there was no problem; nobody really wanted to wipe out the single-sex nature of these organizations, and that took care of the problem for the time being. Of course, we can certainly recognize such an exemption would become unconstitutional under ERA. If you have a constitutional amendment, you are stuck with it, all over the nation and you've got to take it all down the line in all of these aspects.

Now we see another variation of this in the matter of college and school athletics. HEW has been regulating with the athletic implementation of this Act, and they have now come forth with some regulations. And you may or may not agree with the specifics of it, but they apply what some people might consider a rational approach to the problem. They address women's athletics and say they can compete in non-contact sports, the women have the right to compete with the men. But they do make the provision that, in contact sports, no college or high school is compelled to put girls and boys on the same team.

Now, that type of rational approach is possible at the present time, but now contrast that with what you get under the Equal Rights Amendment. We have a beautiful illustration of that in the state of Pennsylvania, where they have passed a state Equal Rights Amendment and are already beginning to feel the effects. Just a few weeks ago, the Pennsylvania courts handed down a decision on the state Equal Rights Amendment which mandated every high school in the state of Pennsylvania to permit girls and boys to compete and practice together in all contact sports, specifically including football and wrestling. And this was done under the Equal Rights Amendment and it is mandatory under the Equal Rights Amendment. Now, please note the decision did not say that the school has to have a girls' football team and a girls' wrestling team if you have a boys' team; they would have to compete together. And, this is the co-ed nature, the gender-free nature, that is required by the Equal Rights Amendment, and we have this perfect example in the state of Pennsylvania of what the Equal Rights Amendment requires. I think that this is just a good example of the nonsense and mischief that is invoked when you require everything that is touched by federal law, state law, the educational systems, public funding, or administrative regulations to be absolutely gender-free. It is the default to every question of the law up and down the line.

Now let's move for a moment from the educational institutions that get public aid to the private schools and see what it's like if we add all girls. There was a Supreme Court decision about a year ago that is relevant to this discussion. Internal Revenue handed down a regulation a couple of years ago that said that any school—private school, that is—which discriminated in its admissions on the basis of race cannot tie up a tax-exempt status. Now, the school in question was a private religious school that did not get any federal aid. But, of course, a private school has a benefit which is known as tax exemption. And Internal Revenue said you can't be tax-exempt if you discriminate on the basis of race, and this ruling was upheld by the Supreme Court. Now, I don't happen to agree with that school rule, but I want you to consider what this will mean when a similar ruling is applied to discrimination on the basis of sex, implying that it becomes absolutely clear that no private school, even if it takes no federal aid, would be permitted to function as a single–sex school—as an all-girls or all-boys school—because, by their definition, such schools discriminate on the basis of sex. And while there are not too many at the college level, there are many more at the secondary level.

And I ask the ERA proponent lawyers if this will be the result, they say, "Yes, it will be the result, and we want it to be the result, because we don't think any educational institution should have the right to discriminate on the basis of sex and still hold tax-exempt status." So, if you want to make all educational institutions at every level, private or public, co-ed, mandated co-ed under federal regulation, ERA would surely do that. Then I saw a senator at this particular hearing ask the proponent lawyer the next logical step: if ERA would put this to private schools, what about the churches themselves, which hold tax-exempt status also? And she hesitated, and didn't care to commit herself one way or the other on the effect that ERA would have on the churches.

Well, I think the logic of this is compelling. We know that the women's liberation movement is making a strong rise at the present time against churches that discriminate on the basis of sex. And while we hold discrimination on the basis of sex, some others have called it simply assigning a different role to men and women in their functions honoring family units. The women's lib movement is making a special drive to force the churches to ordain women as clergy. And they are trying to force the women to go into the seminaries, and into theological institutions and to give them financial aid to get them in, and they will lose their tax exemption if they don't do it. Now, this is certainly one of their objectives.

Now, the tough question is that they look upon the Equal Rights Amendment as the Constitutional basis for litigation to achieve that goal. And that is what they'll do, because this judge will give them the means to litigate toward their objective. Now, there are some churches today that are ordaining women, and they're right to do so; I fully support their right to do that if that is their choice. But there are other churches that do not care to ordain women, and I do not feel that we should give to the Internal Revenue the power to withdraw their tax exemption if they do not.

Let's move onto some other issues. First of all, the right to be exempted from the draft. Now we seem to fight in these foreign wars about every ten years—the politicians keep promising peace, but we keep having these wars about every ten years—and all young men aged eighteen have to register for the draft. You know that if you don't register for the draft, you go to jail—several hundred young men went to jail last year because they didn't register—and the most immediate thing that will happen if the Equal Rights Amendment is ratified is that every eighteen-year-old girl will be compelled to sign up, register, get a draft number, be part of the lottery system and be available for call. Now this is not what the majority of American women want. The way they line up the support of these women's organizations, they'll go into a uniformed women's group, and they will handle this issue like this: they will say, "Oh, you don't think Congress will really draft women, do you?" Or they will say, "All of the women will not be drafted." Well, now those are sleazy arguments, that's it. Nobody ever said all women will be drafted; obviously, if you're over age and you only have one eye and one leg you're not going to be drafted. I want you to get the hypocrisy of these types of arguments. In the past, Congress has accepted all married men; the ERA would require it to extend to all married women as well. Now, there are a few people in this audience that can remember back to World War II; they know that men up through age 35 were drafted and put into combat, and then there's nothing in ERA that says you don't draft married men or married women; all the ERA does, it says you have to treat the sexes equally; and that is, if the national emergencies call for the draft of married men and fathers and placing them into combat in some South Pacific jungle, then married women and mothers would have to be treated exactly the same. All ERA requires is a quota.

Now, when these ERA proponents come into the legislative hearing they sing a different tune. They don't put out this stuff of, "Oh you don't think Congress will really draft women, do you?" Oh, no, they don't think they have to say that to the legislators and lawyers there, so they take an entirely different package. They come in and say, "We want women drafted and we want women put into combat, and we don't think women will get their equal and full rights in our society until they are treated absolutely equally to men." And I heard one legislator ask one of these proponents, "Well, if we draft women, couldn't you give all the women the desk jobs, the safe jobs, and leave the fighting up to the men?" And she replied, "Oh, no, because that would discriminate against women and deprive us of our equal opportunity to win a Congressional Medal of Honor."

Now let's move onto another subject, and that is the takeaway of the rights of the wives. One of the great things about the country we live in is that it is a society that respects the family as the basic unit. And we have many laws at the state and federal level which are designed to hold the family together. Now, maybe there's some better way that civilization will sometime discover for living together in a civilized community, but I don't know what it is, and I would like to stick with the family as the basic unit.

Now, what laws reflect as an assumption of our society is the family is what we want for our basic unit. They also reflect the obvious fact that women have babies and men don't have babies. Now, I've had some colleges, they tell me they're working on some other alternatives to that, too, but until I see it, I will also start with that as the fundamental assumption. Now take some of these fundamental assumptions: the laws of every one of our fifty states make it a financial obligation of the husband to support his wife. These are good laws; these are laws designed to keep the family together, laws designed to give the wife the right to be in her home with her own babies because we look upon the fundamental home as a good that we want to protect and encourage. These laws also require the husband to provide a home for his wife in accordance with his pay. These laws and other laws require the husband to be the primary support of his minor children. There are many things that these laws reflect in our legal system. This assumption that the husband has the obligation of support is what enables a married woman who does not have paid employment to take benefits in her husband's name. Why? Because the family is what gives her the right to collect against her husband. These are the laws which enable a woman who has made her career in the home to get social security benefits based on her husband's earnings. Why? Because we recognized this obligation before.

Now, these laws of family and family property vary slightly from state to state; there are a number of states that have certain special and unique privileges and exceptions for widows, because we think of widows as a certain class of people who are entitled to some special financial advantage, and these laws vary from state to state, but they're good laws. Now, when ERA comes along, what ERA does is to make everything equal; no matter what the laws say to do, they've got to treat men and women absolutely equally. And this is the takeaway of the rights that the wife now has. In every incident, it will take away the rights the wife now has; this is why a U.S. Senator calls ERA "the most destructive piece of legislation that has ever passed the United States Congress."

Colorado's ERA had already gone into effect. The first thing that happened in this area was that the Colorado court threw out the family support laws—they said that only husbands could go to jail for not supporting their wives; wives can't go to jail for not supporting their husbands, so that's discriminatory, and they struck it down. And then the Colorado legislature addressed itself to the problem, and they did. What will they require under ERA? And, that is, they struck out the sexist words—now the sexist words are "male," "female," "man," "woman," "husband," and "wife"—and they replaced them with sex-neutral words which are "person" and "spouse." So now the Colorado law names the principle support "spouse." And anyone can plainly see that's not the same thing at all as saying that a husband will support his wife. So now the wife has an equal financial obligation under pain of being convicted as guilty of a class-five felony. So, there is a clause, with normal exceptions made for the wife who is pregnant, or has six children at home, or whatever. It's equality and has to be determined equally.

Pennsylvania's another state with a state ERA; under that, the Pennsylvania courts invalidated the special rights that wives had for maintenance and for payment of lawyer's fees. They said, "That's discriminatory, let's slow radically down, so we should strike them down." Please know they did not extend it to the men, they just struck them down.

The Pennsylvania courts have also invalidated the Pennsylvania law making the father the primary supporter of his minor children; they put the equal financial burden on all the mothers. Now this is equality, and in no way, can you say that this is an advance on the cause of women; it takes away the rights that women now have.

I personally think that if ERA were ratified the ones who will be hurt the most are the senior women—the women who have made being a wife and mother their full-time career, and now no-fault divorce has become rather easy, and if her husband says, "Trade her in for a new model"—she now is being faced with the courts increasingly saying, "This is the age of equality; go out and take care of yourself now." And that is what it is doing to the marriage contract and it is very hurtful to the best interests of women.

Another area it will affect is the area of women and their right to protective labor legislation in the manual labor theater. Now I believe that in professional, academic, or business pursuits, a woman has completely equal labor demands because she's just as smart. But in physical labor a woman cannot compete equally with a man, and it is very unfair to her to put her in a position where the company can push her exactly like a man. It's in recognition of the obvious physical differences between men and women that the state has erected this fabric of protective labor legislation. These are meaningful laws to the women who have nothing to sell in the marketplace but their physical labor. These women don't have careers; they just have jobs, and they're working just because they need the money. And what ERA does is to wipe out the protection that we have formally given them in terms of making them subject to be worked too many hours a day, too many days of the week. Protective labor legislation has mandated certain rest areas, rest periods, chairs to sit down on, sometimes more generous workers' compensation for injuries to more parts of the body for a woman than a man—and these are things that are meaningful to the woman who does manual work. And, don't let anyone tell you that when the courts look at this, they will extend them to the men. That is ridiculous, and has not happened in any single incidence. In every case where the protective labor legislation has been struck down under the Civil Rights Act of 1964, the women have lost it and the men have not gained it.

Now there are all kinds of additional endless mischief and nonsense the ERA is going to cause, and I came upon one recently that I think illustrates this. There was a financial commentator, columnist, named Sylvia Porter, whose column appeared in the newspapers across the country—I don't know if she appears here, but she's very well-respected as a syndicated columnist in Money Matters. She recently said in one of her columns that there was a bill before Congress to require husbands to pay social security taxes on their wives who were in the home and did not have paid employment. And, she said, in some length to argue, that this would require the husbands to pay double social security taxes, and that is true; it would be double. But after all, if you have to hire somebody to do the housework, you would have to pay social security on her; therefore, it's only right that he would have to pay social security taxes on his wife. Now, in the words of Senator Sanders, "Whether or not this bill passes, the Equal Rights Amendment, when ratified, will require it."

Now, just think over what this means. I have seen a wide range of estimates as to what the worth of a housewife is; they all started about $12,000 a year and go up. Now it's unclear whether the husband is going to have to pay social security taxes on his wife at the eight percent rate of self-employed persons or at a 5.6 percent rate of people you employ plus an additional 5.6 percent paid by the husband as the employer. But in any event, it would probably figure out to about $960 per year in additional taxes that the husband would have to pay on his wife who does not have paid employment. And, of course, with this additional tax, he will not get any additional benefits because the wife already has the right to draw Social Security benefits based on her husband's earnings. So, if anyone tells you that ERA is going to give new dignity to the housewife, just remember that this "new dignity" is going to cost you those $960 per year in additional taxes. And there are more accounts of people in our country today that are already paid for with social security taxes than they are with income taxes.

Another aspect of the Equal Rights Amendment is Section II. Section II says Congress will have the power to enforce it by appropriate legislation. This is the grab for power at the federal level. This is what they'll take off the hands of the state legislatures, make new areas of jurisdiction that the federal government hasn't yet got its meddling fingers into, including marriage, marriage private law, divorce and child custody—at any time in the legislation, it makes a difference between men and women. Why anybody would want to give a whole batch of jurisdiction to the federal government when it can't begin to solve the problems we have now is more than I can understand. I can't think of the reason why we can find so many people on the federal payroll who are working, lobbying, scraping and testifying in behalf of the Equal Rights Amendment. They have been doing it for years on your tax money. Time and again, when I go out to speak at hearings, I have to pay my plane fare. I chide my opponents as they spend your tax money. They testify before state legislatures for biddings, they do television debates, they travel all around the country speaking to organizations, they use telephone calling all over the country. They hold lengthy sessions for employees on government time to tell them why they ought to support the Equal Rights Amendment. Those who are for the Equal Rights Amendment are not for equal rights. They have to get ready all these expensive booklets at taxpayers' expense—they only come out in Washington—and they have all this money to spend; and in the division of money they have many other sources; you know they hire the top political consulting firms in the country to push ERA in the states that have not yet ratified it. They have other sources, too; the Rockefeller Foundation gave $288,000 to the Status of Women Council in California, which was announced to be used for ERA nationally. And millions of dollars from the *Playboy* magazine—that is what happened in the ERA efforts. This is another example of the hypocrisy of the proponents; they try to take the position that they're against people treating women as sex objects like the *Playboy* magazine, but they certainly are quite willing to take *Playboy* money under the table. This is just one more example of the hypocrisy and the difference in the message that the proponents give depending on which type of group they are talking to; you get more truth when you get them at a state legislative hearing than when they have to be subject to cross examination.

So here are a couple reasons why the momentum is on our side. Last year, the support was 8–3 in our favor; three states ratified, seven states rejected, and one state rescinded its previous ratification. This year, the score is 14–1 in our favor; one ratified, but fourteen state legislatures rejected the Equal Rights Amendment. The momentum is all against the Equal Rights Amendment and what it will do, they recognize that. But on the other hand, it is a big takeaway of the rights we now have, and they are coming out in droves in state after state asking the legislatures to rescind their previous ratification and to reject them in the states that have not yet ratified.

Thank you very much.

Elizabeth Cady Stanton (1815–1902)

"As to woman's subjection, on which both the [biblical] canon and the civil law delight to dwell, it is important to note that equal dominion is given to woman over every living thing, but not one word is said giving man dominion over woman."[6]

By any standard, Elizabeth Cady Stanton is an icon for the American feminist movement. This quote, from *The Woman's Bible*—written to counter all scriptures interpreted to denigrate women from the pulpit and courtroom—is from Stanton's commentary on Genesis 1, describing how man and woman both bear the image of God. During her lifetime struggle for women's rights, she challenged orthodox religious teaching about women's subordination, as well as civil law that reinforced women's inferiority.

A mother of seven children, Stanton was a tireless and unapologetic advocate for women's rights. Stanton's noteworthy accomplishments include "The Declaration of Rights and Sentiments" (1848), a manifesto

of equality, and being one of the primary organizers of the first wom-
en's rights convention in Seneca Falls, New York. "The Sentiments" is
patterned after the Declaration of Independence and was signed by
sixty-eight women and thirty-two men at the Seneca Falls convention.
She argued for women's equality as part of natural law.

The address, "The Solitude," was delivered at the end of her feminist activism when Stanton was seventy-six years old. It was offered
twice on the same day: first to the House Judiciary Committee and then
to the National American Woman Suffrage Association Convention.
Unlike her other speeches advocating specific feminist reforms, this
speech grounds the basis for all human rights in the "Protestant" idea
of the individual conscience and the "republican" idea of citizenship.
This speech surpasses appeals for specific legislative reforms and calls
for the naked recognition of each solitary soul's transcendent value.
The central message of equal rights based on the dignity and self-sovereignty of each individual resonates today.

Stanton opens with four main points. First, she argues that a
woman, as an individual is "the arbiter of her own destiny," meaning
that her rights include all that is necessary to take responsibility for her
own life.

Second, she states that women as citizens should have the same
rights as other citizens.

Third, Stanton says, that a woman is responsible for her own "individual happiness and development," and so must have the means to
enact her rights and duties. Fourth, she posits that a woman's prior-
ity to herself as an individual supersedes her roles as "mother, wife,
sister, daughter." This point argues against any discussion about wom-
en's rights and separate spheres. Her strongest argument, she says,
for women to share in all opportunities, is "the solitude and personal
responsibility of her own individual life," shared by every human soul.
"To guide our own craft," Stanton proclaims, "we must be captain,
pilot, engineer, with chart and compass to stand at the wheel [...] It
matters not whether the solitary voyager is man or woman."

The speaker proceeds to describe different places in life where individuals face their own solitude and need to be equipped and rightly

educated for self-sovereignty: as a lonely child, a disappointed young person, the prisoner and the king, the wife and mother, and elder. Stanton refers to the solitude of Jesus Christ in the passion of Gethsemane, trial before Pilate, betrayal of his disciples, and the agonies of the cross.

Her parting challenge is this: "Who, I ask you, can dare take, on himself the rights, the duties, the responsibilities of another human soul?"

* * *

"The Solitude of Self" (1892)[7]

Washington, D.C.

January 18, 1892

Mr. Chairman and gentlemen of the committee:

We have been speaking before Committees of the Judiciary for the last twenty years, and we have gone over all the arguments in favor of a sixteenth amendment which are familiar to all you gentlemen; therefore, it will not be necessary that I should repeat them again.

The point I wish plainly to bring before you on this occasion is the individuality of each human soul; our Protestant idea, the right of individual conscience and judgment—our republican idea, individual citizenship. In discussing the rights of woman, we are to consider, first, what belongs to her as an individual, in a world of her own, the arbiter of her own destiny, an imaginary Robinson Crusoe with her woman Friday on a solitary island. Her rights under such circumstances are to use all her faculties for her own safety and happiness.

Secondly, if we consider her as a citizen, as a member of a great nation, she must have the same rights as all other members, according to the fundamental principles of our Government.

Thirdly, viewed as a woman, an equal factor in civilization, her rights and duties are still the same—individual happiness and development.

Fourthly, it is only the incidental relations of life, such as mother, wife, sister, daughter, that may involve some special duties and training. In the usual discussion in regard to woman's sphere, such men as Herbert Spencer, Frederic Harrison, and Grant Allen uniformly subordinate her rights and duties as an individual, as a citizen, as a woman, to the necessities of these incidental relations, some of which a large class of women may never assume. In discussing the sphere of man, we do not decide his rights as an individual, as a citizen, as a man by his duties as a father, a husband, a brother, or a son, relations some of which he may never fill. Moreover, he would be better fitted for these very relations and whatever special work he might choose to do to earn his bread by the complete development of all his faculties as an individual.

Just so with woman. The education that will fit her to discharge the duties in the largest sphere of human usefulness will best fit her for whatever special work she may be compelled to do.

The isolation of every human soul and the necessity of self-dependence must give each individual the right, to choose his own surroundings.

The strongest reason for giving woman all the opportunities for higher education, for the full development of her faculties, forces of mind and body; for giving her the most enlarged freedom of thought and action; a complete emancipation from all forms of bondage, of custom, dependence, superstition; from all the crippling influences of fear, is the solitude and personal responsibility of her own individual life. The strongest reason why we ask for woman a voice in the government under which she lives; in the religion she is asked to believe; equality in social life, where she is a chief factor; a place in the trades and professions, where she may earn her bread, is because of her birthright to self-sovereignty; because, as an individual, she must rely on herself. No matter how much women prefer to lean, to be protected and supported, nor how much men desire to have them do so, they must make the voyage of life alone, and for safety in an emergency they must know something of the laws of navigation. To guide our own craft, we must be captain, pilot, engineer; with chart and compass to stand at the wheel; to watch the wind and waves and know when to take in the sail, and to read the signs in the firmament over all. It matters not whether the solitary voyager is man or woman.

Nature having endowed them equally, leaves them to their own skill and judgment in the hour of danger, and, if not equal to the occasion, alike they perish.

To appreciate the importance of fitting every human soul for independent action, think for a moment of the immeasurable solitude of self. We come into the world alone, unlike all who have gone before us; we leave it alone under circumstances peculiar to ourselves. No mortal ever has been, no mortal ever will be like the soul just launched on the sea of life. There can never again be just such a combination of prenatal influences; never again such environments as make up the infancy, youth, and manhood of this one. Nature never repeats herself, and the possibilities of one human soul will never be found in another. No one has ever found two blades of ribbon grass alike, and no one will ever find two human beings alike. Seeing, then, what must be the infinite diversity in human character, we can in a measure appreciate the loss to a nation when any large class of the people is uneducated and unrepresented in the government. We ask for the complete development of every individual, first, for his own benefit and happiness. In fitting out an army we give each soldier his own knapsack, arms, powder, his blanket, cup, knife, fork and spoon. We provide alike for all their individual necessities, then each man bears his own burden.

Again, we ask complete individual development for the general good; for the consensus of the competent on the whole round of human interest; on all questions of national life, and here each man must bear his share of the general burden. It is sad to see how soon friendless children are left to bear their own burdens before they can analyze their feelings; before they can even tell their joys and sorrows, they are thrown on their own resources. The great lesson that nature seems to teach us at all ages is self-dependence, self-protection, self-support. What a touching instance of a child's solitude; of that hunger of the heart for love and recognition, in the case of the little girl who helped to dress a Christmas tree for the children of the family in which she served. On finding there was no present for herself she slipped away in the darkness and spent the night in an open field sitting on a stone, and when found in the morning was weeping as if her heart would break. No mortal will ever know the thoughts that passed through the mind of that friendless child in the long hours of that cold night, with only the silent stars to keep her company. The mention of her case in the daily papers moved many generous hearts to send her presents, but in the hours of her keenest sufferings she was thrown wholly on herself for consolation.

In youth our most bitter disappointments, our brightest hopes and ambitions are known only to ourselves; even our friendship and love we never fully share with another; there is something of every passion in every situation we conceal. Even so in our triumphs and our defeats.

The successful candidate for the Presidency and his opponent each have a solitude peculiarly his own, and good form forbids either in speak of his pleasure or regret. The solitude of the king on his throne and the prisoner in his cell differs in character and degree, but it is solitude nevertheless.

We ask no sympathy from others in the anxiety and agony of a broken friendship or shattered love. When death sunders our nearest ties, alone we sit in the shadow of our affliction. Alike mid the greatest triumphs and darkest tragedies of life we walk alone. On the divine heights of human attainments, eulogized and worshiped as a hero or saint, we stand alone. In ignorance, poverty, and vice, as a pauper or criminal, alone we starve or steal; alone we suffer the sneers and rebuffs of our fellows; alone we are hunted and hounded through dark courts and alleys, in by-ways and highways; alone we stand in the judgment seat; alone in the prison cell we lament our crimes and misfortunes; alone we expiate them on the gallows. In hours like these we realize the awful solitude of individual life, its pains, its penalties, its responsibilities; hours in which the youngest and most helpless are thrown on their own resources for guidance and consolation. Seeing then that life must ever be a march and a battle, that each soldier must be equipped for his own protection, it is the height of cruelty to rob the individual of a single natural right.

To throw obstacles in the way of a complete education is like putting out the eyes; to deny the rights of property, like cutting off the hands. To deny political equality is to rob the ostracized of all self-respect; of credit in the market place; of recompense in the world of work; of a voice in those who make and administer the law; a choice in the jury before whom they are tried, and in the judge who decides their punishment. Shakespeare's play of Titus and Andronicus contains a terrible satire on woman's position in the nineteenth century: "Rude men," (the play tells us) "seized the king's daughter, cut out her tongue, cut off her hands, and then bade her go call for water and wash her hands." What a picture of woman's position. Robbed of her natural rights, handicapped by law and custom at every turn, yet compelled to fight her own battles, and in the emergencies of life to fall back on herself for protection.

The girl of sixteen, thrown on the world to support herself, to make her own place in society, to resist the temptations that surround her and maintain a spotless integrity, must do all this by native force or superior education. She does not acquire this power by being trained to trust others and distrust herself. If she wearies of the struggle, finding it hard work to swim upstream, and allows herself to drift with the current, she will find plenty of company, but not one to share her misery in the hour of her deepest humiliation. If she tried to retrieve her position, to conceal the past, her life is hedged about with fears lest willing hands should tear the veil from what she fain would hide. Young and friendless, *she* knows the bitter solitude of self.

How the little courtesies of life on the surface of society, deemed so important from man towards woman, fade into utter insignificance in view of the deeper tragedies in which she must play her part alone, where no human aid is possible.

The young wife and mother, at the head of some establishment with a kind husband to shield her from the adverse winds of life, with wealth, fortune and position, has a certain harbor of safety, secure against the ordinary ills of life. But to manage a household, have a desirable influence in society, keep her friends and the affections of her husband, train her children and servants well, she must have rare common sense, wisdom, diplomacy, and a knowledge of human nature. To do all this she needs the cardinal virtues and the strong points of character that the most successful statesman possesses.

An uneducated woman, trained to dependence, with no resources in herself must make a failure of any position in life. But society says women do not need a knowledge of the world; the liberal training that experience in public life must give, all the advantages of collegiate education; but when for the lack of all this, the woman's happiness is wrecked, alone she bears her humiliation; and the solitude of the weak and the ignorant is indeed pitiable in the wild chase for the prizes of life they are ground to powder.

In age, when the pleasures of youth are passed, children grown up, married and gone, the hurry and hustle of life in a measure over, when the hands are weary of active service, when the old armchair and the fireside are the chosen resorts, then men and women alike must fall back on their own resources. If they cannot find companionship in books, if they have no interest in the vital questions of the hour, no interest in watching the consummation of reforms, with which they might have been identified, they soon pass into their dotage. The more fully the faculties of the mind are developed and kept in use, the longer the period of vigor and active interest in all around us continues. If from a lifelong participation in public affairs a woman feels responsible for the laws regulating our system of education, the discipline of our jails and prisons, the sanitary conditions of our private homes, public buildings, and thoroughfares, an interest in commerce, finance, our foreign relations, in any or all of these questions, here solitude will at least be respectable, and she will not be driven to gossip or scandal for entertainment.

The chief reason for opening to every soul the doors to the whole round of human duties and pleasures is the individual development thus attained, the resources thus provided under all circumstances to mitigate the solitude that at times must come to everyone. I once asked Prince Kropotkin, the Russian nihilist, how he endured his long years in prison, deprived of books, pen, ink, and paper. "Ah," he said, "I thought out many questions in which I had a deep interest. In the pursuit of an idea I took no note of time. When tired of solving knotty problems I recited all the beautiful passages in prose or verse I have ever learned. I became acquainted with myself and my own resources. I had a world of my own, a vast empire, that no Russian jailor or Czar could invade." Such is the value of liberal thought and broad culture when shut off from all human companionship, bringing comfort and sunshine within even the four walls of a prison cell.

As women ofttimes share a similar fate, should they not have all the consolation that the most liberal education can give? Their suffering in the prisons of St. Petersburg; in the long, weary marches to Siberia, and in the mines, working side by side with men, surely call for all the self-support that the most exalted sentiments of heroism can give. When suddenly roused at midnight, with the startling cry of "fire! fire!" to find the house over their heads in flames, do women wait for men to point the way to safety? And are the men, equally bewildered and half suffocated with smoke, in a position to do more than try to save themselves?

At such times the most timid women have shown a courage and heroism in saving their husbands and children that has surprised everybody. Inasmuch, then, as woman shares equally the joys and sorrows of time and eternity, is it not the height of presumption in man to propose to represent her at the ballot box and the throne of grace, do her voting in the state, her praying in the church, and to assume the position of high priest at the family altar?

Nothing strengthens the judgment and quickens the conscience like individual responsibility. Nothing adds such dignity to character as the recognition of one's self-sovereignty; the right to an equal place, every where conceded; a place earned by personal merit, not an artificial attainment, by inheritance, wealth, family, and position. Seeing, then that the responsibilities of life rests equally on man and woman, that their destiny is the same, they need the same preparation for time and eternity. The talk of sheltering woman from the fierce storms of life is the sheerest mockery, for they beat on her from every point of the compass, just as they do on man, and with more fatal results, for he has been trained to protect himself, to resist, to conquer. Such are the facts in human experience, the responsibilities of individual sovereignty. Rich and poor, intelligent and ignorant, wise and foolish, virtuous and vicious, man and woman, it is ever the same, each soul must depend wholly on itself.

Whatever the theories may be of woman's dependence on man, in the supreme moments of her life he can not bear her burdens. Alone she goes to the gates of death to give life to every man that is born into the world. No one can share her fears, no one mitigate her pangs; and if her sorrow is greater than she can bear, alone she passes beyond the gates into the vast unknown. From the mountain tops of Judea, long ago, a heavenly voice bade His disciples, "Bear ye one another's burdens," but humanity has not yet risen to that point of self-sacrifice, and if ever so willing, how few the burdens are that one soul can bear for another. In the highways of Palestine; in prayer and fasting on the solitary mountain top; in the Garden of Gethsemane; before the judgment seat of Pilate; betrayed by one of His trusted disciples at His last supper; in His agonies on the cross, even Jesus of Nazareth, in these last sad days on earth, felt the awful solitude of self. Deserted by man, in agony he cries, "My God! My God! why hast Thou forsaken me?" And so it ever must be in the conflicting scenes of life, on the long weary march, each one walks alone. We may have many friends, love, kindness, sympathy and charity to smoothe our pathway in everyday life, but in the tragedies and triumphs of human experience each moral stands alone.

But when all artificial trammels are removed, and women are recognized as individuals, responsible for their own environments, thoroughly educated for all the positions in life they may be called to fill; with all the resources in themselves that liberal thought and broad culture can give; guided by their own conscience and judgment; trained to self-protection by a healthy development of the muscular system and skill in the use of weapons of defense, and stimulated to self-support by a knowledge of the business world and the pleasure that pecuniary independence must ever give; when women are trained in this way they will, in a measure, be fitted for those hours of solitude that come alike to all, whether prepared or otherwise. As in our extremity we must depend on ourselves, the dictates of wisdom point of complete individual development.

In talking of education how shallow the argument that each class must be educated for the special work it proposed to do, and all those faculties not needed in this special work must lie dormant and utterly wither for want of use, when, perhaps, these will be the very faculties needed in life's greatest emergencies. Some say, Where is the use of drilling girls in the languages, the sciences, in law, medicine, theology? As wives, mothers, housekeepers, cooks, they need a different curriculum from boys who are to fill all positions. The chief cooks in our great hotels and ocean steamers are men. In our large cities men run the bakeries; they make our bread, cake and pies. They manage the laundries; they are now considered our best milliners and dressmakers. Because some men fill these departments of usefulness, shall we regulate the curriculum in Harvard and Yale to their present necessities? If not, [then] why this talk in our best colleges of a curriculum for girls who are crowding into the trades and professions; teachers in all our public schools, rapidly filling many lucrative and honorable positions in life? They are showing too, their calmness and courage in the most trying hours of human experience.

You have probably all read in the daily papers of the terrible storm in the Bay of Biscay when a tidal wave made such havoc on the shore, wrecking vessels, unroofing houses and carrying destruction everywhere. Among other buildings the woman's prison was demolished. Those who escaped saw men struggling to reach the shore. They promptly by clasping hands made a chain of themselves and pushed out into the sea, again and again, at the risk of their lives, until they had brought six men to shore, carried them to a shelter, and did all in their power for their comfort and protection.

What special school training could have prepared these women for this sublime moment of their lives? In times like this humanity rises above all college curriculums and recognises Nature as the greatest of all teachers in the hour of danger and death. Women are already the equals of men in the whole of realm of thought, in art, science, literature, and government. With telescopic vision they explore the starry firmament and bring back the history of the planetary world. With chart and compass they pilot ships across the mighty deep, and with skillful finger send electric messages around the globe. In galleries of art the beauties of nature and the virtues of humanity are immortalized by them on canvas and by their inspired touch dull blocks of marble are transformed into angels of light.

In music they speak again the language of Mendelssohn, Beethoven, Chopin, Schumann, and are worthy interpreters of their great thoughts. The poetry and novels of the century are theirs, and they have touched the keynote of reform in religion, politics, and social life. They fill the editor's and professor's chair, and plead at the bar of justice, walk the wards of the hospital, and speak from the pulpit and the platform; such is the type of womanhood that an enlightened public sentiment welcomes today, and such the triumph of the facts of life over the false theories of the past.

Is it, then, consistent to hold the developed woman of this day within the same narrow political limits as the dame with the spinning wheel and knitting needle occupied in the past? No! No! Machinery has taken the labors of woman as well as man on its tireless shoulders; the loom and the spinning wheel are but dreams of the past; the pen, the brush, the easel, the chisel, have taken their places, while the hopes and ambitions of women are essentially changed. We see reason sufficient in the outer conditions of human beings for individual liberty and development, but when we consider the self dependence of every human soul we see the need of courage, judgment, and the exercise of every faculty of mind and body, strengthened and developed by use, in woman as well as man.

Whatever may be said of man's protecting power in ordinary conditions, mid all the terrible disasters by land and sea, in the supreme moments of danger, alone woman must ever meet the horrors of the situation; the Angel of Death even makes no royal pathway for her. Man's love and sympathy enter only into the sunshine of our lives. In that solemn solitude of self, that links us with the immeasurable and the eternal, each soul lives alone forever. A recent writer says:

I remember once, in crossing the Atlantic, to have gone upon the deck of the ship at midnight, when a dense black cloud enveloped the sky, and the great deep was roaring madly under the lashes of demoniac winds. My feeling was not of danger or fear (which is a base surrender of the immortal soul), but of utter desolation and loneliness; a little speck of life shut in by a tremendous darkness. Again I remember to have climbed the slopes of the Swiss Alps, up beyond the point where vegetation ceases, and the stunted conifers no longer struggle against the unfeeling blasts. Around me lay a huge confusion of rocks, out of which the gigantic ice peaks shot into the measureless blue of the heavens, and again my only feeling was the awful solitude. And yet, there is a solitude, which each and every one of us has always carried with him more inaccessible than the ice-cold mountains, more profound than the midnight sea; the solitude of self. Our inner being, which we call ourself, no eye nor touch of man or angel has ever pierced. It is more hidden than the caves of the gnome; the sacred adytum of the oracle; the hidden chamber of eleusinian mystery, for to it only omniscience is permitted to enter.

Such is individual life. Who, I ask you, can take, dare take, on himself the rights, the duties, the responsibilities of another human soul?

Notes

1   Adrienne E. Christiansen, "Clarina Howard Nichols (1810–1855): A Modest Voice for Woman's Rights," in *Women Public Speakers in the United States, 1800–1925: A Bio-critical Sourcebook*, ed. Karlyn Kohrs Campbell (Westport, CT: Greenwood Press, 1993), 258.

2   Clarina Howard Nichols, "The Responsibilities of a Woman" (speech, Second Annual Woman's Rights Convention, Worcester, New York, October 1851), SoJust (EdChange), accessed March 1, 2018, http://www.sojust.net/speeches/nichols_responsibilities.html

3   Phyllis Schlafly, "The Positive Woman's Movement," in *Phyllis Schlafly Speaks, Volume 1: Her Favorite Speeches*, ed. Ed Martin (Skellig America, 2016), 221–233. Used by permission.

4   Ibid.

5   Phyllis Schlafly, "The Equal Rights Amendment," in *Phyllis Schlafly Speaks, Volume 1: Her Favorite Speeches* ed. Ed Martin (Skellig America, 2016), 32–56.

6 Elizabeth Cady Stanton, *The Woman's Bible* (Seattle: Seattle Coalition Taskforce on Women and Religion, 1974), 15.

7 Elizabeth Cady Stanton, "Solitude of Self" (speech, House Judiciary Committee, Washington, D.C., February 18 1982), Voices of Democracy, accessed March 1, 2018, http://voicesofdemocracy.umd.edu/the-solitude-of-self-speech-by-ecs-to-the-house-judiciary-committee-speech-text/

Education

Education, literacy, and learning are keystones to human freedom in all societies. However, in many countries, girls' opportunities to go to school are limited or non-existent. Some religious leaders teach that girls should not receive an education because they might rebel against their God-ordained roles as submissive wives and mothers and that formal education is not needed to fulfill these divinely sanctioned responsibilities. Sometimes, this prohibition against girls' education can lead to violence, as in the example of Malala Yousafzai. At age fifteen, she was shot in the head while on her way to school.[1] After a remarkable recovery, she is now an international symbol of freedom and the youngest person to win the Nobel Peace Prize.

Early marriage can also limit girls' continuing education. Furthermore, some families simply cannot afford to pay for the education of both their sons and daughters, so their sons get to go to school. Whatever the causes preventing women and girls from learning, access to education is a strong theme and transcendent value for these speakers who understand its importance to equality. In this section, we study the speech texts of two women from different time periods, with the same message. Each speaks passionately about the importance of education to foster equality and a better life for all.

First, in "Why Sit Ye Here and Die?" African American abolitionist Maria W. Stewart contends to her mixed-race, mixed-gender audience in Franklin Hall Boston, September 21, 1932, that free Black women deserve to be educated because "[they] must rise to that degree of respectability that true merit deserves" and not be limited to servile "professions resembling slavery." Further, using numerous biblical passages easily recognizable to her Christian discourse community, she argues from the example of Jesus Christ. Many consider Stewart the first African American woman to make a public address.

The second speech, from educator and presidential advisor Dr. Mary Bethune McLeod, recounts the progress and contributions African Americans have made to American life in literature, agriculture and other fields. In this brief radio address, Bethune also calls for greater freedoms in voting, along with additional educational and occupational opportunities for African American so that all citizens can participate in the promise of to come. Her address on democracy is grounded in her transcendent values of deep Christian faith, human equality, and her belief in democracy. Bethune's life is a beacon of life-long dedication to the value of education as a basic human right. Today, her legacy lives on in the Bethune-Cookman University that educates young women and men for service and leadership.

Maria W. Stewart (1803–1879)

"Methinks there are no chains so galling as those that bind the soul, and exclude it from the vast field of useful and scientific knowledge."

Maria W. Stewart embodies the oft-used phrase "speaking truth to power." As an abolitionist, lecturer, and women's rights activist, Stewart declared that the lack of education for African-American women and men living "free" in the North was equivalent to slavery in the South. Her address to the New England Anti-Slavery Society in Boston's Franklin Hall on September 21, 1832, passionately challenged her mixed-race, mixed-gender, "promiscuous" audience not only to oppose slavery but also to advocate for African American women to receive opportunities a better life through education "which true merit deserves."

Maria W. Stewart was born 1803 in Connecticut and orphaned at age five. She married James W. Stewart after serving a ministerial family as an indentured servant and paid servant. Her own education consisted of "Sabbath" schools under the auspices of the church. Tragically, her husband James died just three years after they wed. As one of the few free middle-class Blacks in the north, Maria experienced a Christian conversion and a divine call to speak up to "take off the reproach that is cast on people of color." Between the whites who swindled her out of her widow's inheritance, her own experiences and the death of another supportive abolitionist, Stewart emerged as a devout advocate for women's rights. She was particularly propelled by her Christian sense of justice for African Americans.

The title of her address is an allusion to 2 Kings 7:3–4 in which African Americans are compared to the story of four lepers waiting for either certain death or mercy at the hands of their oppressors. As in this example, Stewart uses frequent biblical references as analogies to support her arguments. The tone of her address is in the confrontational Old Testament tradition of prophets like Jeremiah warning of coming judgment. To the modern reader, her speech seems quite contemporary with voices calling for racial equality. She has a colorful, artful style to describe the plight of those confined to a life of manual labor and servitude due to lack of education and white prejudice.

While she gives credit to those who want to live in service, she appeals to this audience who claim to be the champions of freedom to consider the young women in the kitchens, the young men as the "humblest laborers," the weary toil of middle-aged men and women living in abject poverty, and "aged sires" with wood saws on their backs at age seventy. Speaking of religion in her oratory, Stewart compares how the death of Christ would be in vain to those who will not receive God's mercy to the vanity of those in her audience who speak of freedom and yet do nothing to raise Africa's sons and daughters.

For Stewart, the transcendent value of American equality was common to her audience as a discourse community, and this value is relevant to the state of African Americans servile work and terrible living conditions. Her message—and its warrant—is that the promoters of freedom must additionally advocate for the education of African Americans in order that they might pursue the better life that their value of freedom demands. The consequence, if nothing is accomplished, is for young and old Black girls and women, boys and men to live lives of servitude and to die without the hope of a better life.

Stewart gave four public speeches in her life which were later published. She spent the rest of her life working in organizations dedicated to freedom and taught school in New York and Washington, D.C. She also directed the Freedman's Hospital in Washington where she herself later died. Stewart's legacy as the first African American woman to publicly address a mixed audience, her unwavering religious faith, and her stature as civil rights activist and advocate of education for all makes her an important orator and influence for duty and destiny.

* * *

"Why Sit Ye Here and Die?" (1832)[2]

Lecture at Franklin Hall

Boston, Massachusetts

1832

Why sit ye here and die? If we say we will go to a foreign land, the famine and the pestilence are there, and there we shall die. If we sit here, we shall die. Come let us plead our cause before the whites: if they save us alive, we shall live—and if they kill us, we shall but die.

Methinks I heard a spiritual interrogation—"Who shall go forward, and take off the reproach that is cast upon the people of color? Shall it be a woman?" And my heart made this reply, "If it is thy will, be it even so, Lord Jesus!"

I have heard much respecting the horrors of slavery; but may Heaven forbid that the generality of my color throughout these United States should experience any more of its horrors than to be a servant of servants, or hewers of wood and drawers of water! Tell us no more of southern slavery; for with few exceptions, although I may be very erroneous in my opinion, yet I consider our condition but little better than that. Yet, after all, methinks there are no chains so galling as the chains of ignorance—no fetters so binding as those that bind the soul, and exclude it from the vast field of useful and scientific knowledge. O, had I received the advantages of early education, my ideas would, ere now, have expanded far and wide; but, alas! I possess nothing but moral capability—no teachings but the teachings of the Holy Spirit.

I have asked several individuals of my sex, who transact business for themselves, if providing our girls were to give them the most satisfactory references, they would not be willing to grant them an equal opportunity with others? Their reply has been—for their own part, they had no objection; but as it was not the custom, were they to take them into their employ, they would be in danger of losing the public patronage.

And such is the powerful force of prejudice. Let our girls possess what amiable qualities of soul they may; let their characters be fair and spotless as innocence itself; let their natural taste and ingenuity be what they may; it is impossible for scarce an individual of them to rise above the condition of servants. Ah! why is this cruel and unfeeling distinction? Is it merely because God has made our complexion to vary? If it be, O shame to soft, relenting humanity! "Tell it not in Gath! publish it not in the streets of Askelon!" Yet, after all, methinks were the American free people of color to turn their attention more assiduously to moral worth and intellectual improvement, this would be the result: prejudice would gradually diminish, and the whites would be compelled to say, unloose those fetters!

Though black their skins as shades of night,

Their hearts are pure, their souls are white.

Few white persons of either sex, who are calculated for anything else, are willing to spend their lives and bury their talents in performing mean, servile labor. And such is the horrible idea that I entertain respecting a life of servitude, that if I conceived of there being no possibility of my rising above the condition of a servant, I would gladly hail death as a welcome messenger. O, horrible idea, indeed! To possess noble souls aspiring after high and honorable acquirements, yet confined by the chains of ignorance and poverty to lives of continual drudgery and toil. Neither do I know of any who have enriched themselves by spending their lives as house-domestics, washing windows, shaking carpets, brushing boots, or tending upon gentlemen's tables. I can but die for expressing my sentiments; and I am as willing to die by the sword as the pestilence; for I am a true born American; your blood flows in my veins, and your spirit fires my breast.

I observed a piece in *The Liberator* a few months since, stating that the colonizationists had published a work respecting us, asserting that we were lazy and idle. I confute them on that point. Take us generally as a people, we are neither lazy nor idle; and considering how little we have to excite or stimulate us, I am almost astonished that there are so many industrious and ambitious ones to be found; although I acknowledge, with extreme sorrow, that there are some who never were and never will be serviceable to society. And have you not a similar class among yourselves?

Again. It was asserted that we were "a ragged set, crying for liberty." I reply to it, the whites have so long and so loudly proclaimed the theme of equal rights and privileges, that our souls have caught the flame also, ragged as we are. As far as our merit deserves, we feel a common desire to rise above the condition of servants and drudges. I have learnt, by bitter experience, that continual hard labor deadens the energies of the soul, and benumbs the faculties of the mind; the ideas become confined, the mind barren, and, like the scorching sands of Arabia, produces nothing; or, like the uncultivated soil, brings forth thorns and thistles.

Again, continual hard labor irritates our tempers and sours our dispositions; the whole system becomes worn out with toil and fatigue; nature herself becomes almost exhausted, and we care but little whether we live or die. It is true, that the free people of color throughout these United States are neither bought nor sold, nor under the lash of the cruel driver; many obtain a comfortable support; but few, if any, have an opportunity of becoming rich and independent; and the employments we most pursue are as unprofitable to us as the spider's web or the floating bubbles that vanish into air. As servants, we are respected; but let us presume to aspire any higher, our employer regards us no longer. And were it not that the King eternal has declared that Ethiopia shall stretch forth her hands unto God, I should indeed despair.

I do not consider it derogatory, my friends, for persons to live out to service. There are many whose inclination leads them to aspire no higher; and I would highly commend the performance of almost anything for an honest livelihood; but where constitutional strength is wanting, labor of this kind, in its mildest form, is painful. And doubtless many are the prayers that have ascended to Heaven from Africa's daughters for strength to perform their work. Oh, many are the tears that have been shed for the want of that strength! Most of our color have dragged out a miserable existence of servitude from the cradle to the grave. And what literary acquirements can be made, or useful knowledge derived, from either maps, books or charts, by those who continually drudge from Monday morning until Sunday noon? O, ye fairer sisters, whose hands are never soiled, whose nerves and muscles are never strained, go learn by experience! Had we had the opportunity that you have had, to improve our moral and mental faculties, what would have hindered our intellects from being as bright, and our manners from being as dignified as yours? Had it been our lot to have been nursed in the lap of affluence and ease, and to have basked beneath the smiles and sunshine of fortune, should we not have naturally supposed that we were never made to toil? And why are not our forms as delicate, and our constitutions as slender, as yours? Is not the workmanship as curious and complete? Have pity upon us, have pity upon us, O ye who have hearts to feel for "others" woes; for the hand of God has touched us. Owing to the disadvantages under which we labor, there are many flowers among us that are, "...born to bloom unseen, / And waste their fragrance on the desert air."

My beloved brethren, as Christ has died in vain for those who will not accept of offered mercy, so will it be vain for the advocates of freedom to spend their breath in our behalf, unless with united hearts and souls you make some mighty efforts to raise your sons and daughters from the horrible state of servitude and degradation in which they are placed. It is upon you that woman depends; she can do but little besides using her influence; and it is for her sake and yours that I have come forward and made myself a hissing and a reproach among the people; for I am also one of the wretched and miserable daughters of the descendants of fallen Africa. Do you ask, why are you wretched and miserable? I reply, look at many of the most worthy and interesting of us doomed to spend our lives in gentlemen's kitchens.

Look at our young men, smart, active and energetic, with souls filled with ambitious fire; if they look forward, alas! what are their prospects? They can be nothing but the humblest laborers, on account of their dark complexions; hence many of them lose their ambition and become worthless. Look at our middle-aged men, clad in their rusty plaids and coats; in winter, every cent they earn goes to buy their wood and pay their rents; their poor wives also toil beyond their strength, to help support their families.

Look at our aged sires, whose heads are whitened with the frosts of seventy winters, with their old wood-saws on their backs. Alas, what keeps us so? Prejudice, ignorance and poverty. But ah! methinks our oppression is soon to come to an end; yea, before the Majesty of heaven, our groans and cries have reached the ears of the Lord of Sabaoth. As the prayers and tears of Christians will avail the finally impenitent nothing; neither will the prayers and tears of the friends of humanity avail us anything, unless we possess a spirit of virtuous emulation within our breasts. Did the pilgrims, when they first landed on these shores, quietly compose themselves, and say, "the Britons have all the money and all the power, and we must continue their servants forever?" Did they sluggishly sigh and say, "our lot is hard, the Indians own the soil, and we cannot cultivate it?" No; they first made powerful efforts to raise themselves, and then God raised up those illustrious patriots, WASHINGTON and LAFAYETTE, to assist and defend them.

And, my brethren, have you made a powerful effort? Have you prayed the Legislature for mercy's sake to grant you all the rights and privileges of free citizens, that your daughters may rise to that degree of respectability which true merit deserves, and your sons above the servile situations which most of them fill?

Mary McLeod Bethune (1875–1955)

"Our children must never lose their zeal for building a better world. They must not be discouraged from aspiring toward greatness, for they are to be leaders of tomorrow."[3]

Mary McLeod Bethune was a champion for human rights and education for all children, and her legacy endures. In this quote from her last will and testament, Bethune bequeaths to her children love, hope, a thirst for education, faith, racial dignity, a desire to live harmoniously and a responsibility for young people.[4] Born the fifteenth of seventeen children to ex-slaves, Bethune dedicated much of her life to providing educational opportunities for African Americans. Her experience spanned the turbulence of Reconstruction, incidents of lynching and massacre, and the passage of the Fourteenth Amendment. An ardent Christian, Bethune received training from what is now Moody Bible Institute to become a missionary. Instead of going to Africa, she traveled to Augusta, Georgia, and developed a small school into a thriving mission institute for young, Black men and women. Among her many accomplishments, Bethune served three Presidents—Coolidge, Hoover, and, most notably, Franklin D. Roosevelt, as his advisor on minority affairs. Additionally, Daytona Normal & Industrial Institute, which Bethune founded in 1904, later became Bethune–Cookman University and is a thriving institution today.

This short address "What Does American Democracy Mean to Me?" is from America's Town Meeting of the Air, a radio broadcast from New York City aired November 23, 1939. Here Bethune proclaims to this broad NBC audience many of the same themes that Dr. Martin Luther King, Jr., would carry forth almost thirty years later. She grounds the march of democracy in her Christian faith "rising out of the darkness of slavery into the light of freedom" and frequently references the U.S. Constitution. Like King, she grounds the march of civil rights in the American story of freedom. Bethune names literacy, property owner-ship, participation in government, and contributions to culture as evi-dence of how African Americans have embraced this light. Further, she notes the contributions of "labor," "faith," and "song" in education (Booker T. Washington), the arts (James Dunbar and Marion Ander-son), and agriculture (George Washington Carver) as the "first fruits" to the "rich harvest" of further reaping in the fields of freedom.

But, says Bethune, not all doors are open. Lack of educational oppor-tunities, lower levels of work, poverty, fear of lynching, and lack of voting and civil rights are the conditions that common decency and justice will not abide. She argues that African Americans have fought and died for the United States not so much for what "she is, but what we know she can be."

Bethune claims democratic freedom as the transcendent value with education as its means. Her relevant facts include naming the freedoms that African Americans have realized, and the contributions therein made to America. She also names the current conditions faced by many Blacks in servile conditions and lack of opportunity as a consequence of limited access to education and voting rights. She calls for a renewal of commitment to American and the belief in "all she can be" as a true democracy with freedom and opportunity for all.

The possible fight continues for "spiritual awakening" for a free and fearless America, as one nation under God, based on mutual respect and understanding, where all Americans embrace equality. "This dream, this idea, this aspiration, this is what American democ-racy means to me."

* * *

"What Does American Democracy Mean to Me?" (1939)[5]

New York City

1939

Democracy is for me, and for 12 million Black Americans, a goal towards which our nation is marching. It is a dream and an ideal in whose ultimate realization we have a deep and abiding faith. For me, it is based on Christianity, in which we confidently entrust our destiny as a people. Under God's guidance in this great democracy, we are rising out of the darkness of slavery into the light of freedom. Here my race has been afforded [the] opportunity to advance from a people 80 percent illiterate to a people 80 percent literate; from abject poverty to the ownership and operation of a million farms and 750,000 homes; from total disfranchisement to participation in government; from the status of chattels to recognized contributors to the American culture.

As we have been extended a measure of democracy, we have brought to the nation rich gifts. We have helped to build America with our labor, strengthened it with our faith and enriched it with our song. We have given you Paul Lawrence Dunbar, Booker T. Washington, Marian Anderson and George Washington Carver. But even these are only the first fruits of a rich harvest, which will be reaped when new and wider fields are opened to us.

The democratic doors of equal opportunity have not been opened wide to Negroes. In the Deep South, Negro youth is offered only one-fifteenth of the educational opportunity of the average American child. The great masses of Negro workers are depressed and unprotected in the lowest levels of agriculture and domestic service, while the black workers in industry are barred from certain unions and generally assigned to the more laborious and poorly paid work. Their housing and living conditions are sordid and unhealthy. They live too often in terror of the lynch mob; are deprived too often of the Constitutional right of suffrage; and are humiliated too often by the denial of civil liberties. We do not believe that justice and common decency will allow these conditions to continue.

Our faith envisions a fundamental change as mutual respect and understanding between our races come in the path of spiritual awakening. Certainly, there have been times when we may have delayed this mutual understanding by being slow to assume a fuller share of our national responsibility because of the denial of full equality. And yet, we have always been loyal when the ideals of American democracy have been attacked. We have given our blood in its defense—from Crispus Attucks on Boston Commons to the battlefields of France. We have fought for the democratic principles of equality under the law, equality of opportunity, equality at the ballot box, for the guarantees of life, liberty and the pursuit of happiness. We have fought to preserve one nation, conceived in liberty and dedicated to the proposition that all men are created equal. Yes, we have fought for America with all her imperfections, not so much for what she is, but for what we know she can be.

Perhaps the greatest battle is before us, the fight for a new America: fearless, free, united, morally re-armed, in which 12 million Negroes, shoulder to shoulder with their fellow Americans, will strive that this nation under God will have a new birth of freedom, and that government of the people, for the people and by the people shall not perish from the earth. This dream, this idea, this aspiration, this is what American democracy means to me.

Notes

1   As reported first hand in her account in *I am Malala: The Girl Who Stood Up for Education and Was Shot by the Taliban* (London: Weidenfeld & Nicolson, 2013.)

2   Maria W. Stewart, "Why Sit Ye Here and Die?" (speech, Franklin Hall, Boston, MA, September 21, 1832), Voices of Democracy, accessed March 1, 2018, http://voicesofdemocracy.umd.edu/stewart-lecture-delivered-speech-text/

3   Mary McLeod Bethune. "My Last Will and Testament" quoted in Moira Davison Reynolds, *Women Champions of Human Rights: Eleven U.S. Leaders of the Twentieth Century* (Jefferson, NC: McFarland & Company, Inc., 1991), 52–53.

4   Ibid.

5   Mary McLeod Bethune, "What Does American Democracy Mean to Me?" ("America's Town Meeting of the Air," NBC radio broadcast, November 23, 1939), American Public Media, accessed March 1, 2018, http://americanradioworks.publicrdio.org/features/blackspeech/mmbethune.html

Reform

While many speeches in this book argue for change and social reform—in education, voting, abolition, property rights for women, and others—this section focuses on one reforming movement of special merit: prohibition. This social reform serves as an informative case study for women's voices, motivated by religious values, that resulted in change. This case highlights what women can accomplish—even with limited social rights. Grounding this national debate on the social issues of alcohol sales is the idea of True Womanhood, the notion that women, as wives and mothers, were morally superior to their worldly men because they as women served as guardians of the home. Much of the rhetoric of this time echoed this belief as a woman's primary authority to speak. And speak, they did. This argument seems archaic in our modern context, but at the time, this perceived moral authority as "citizen-mothers" fueled the drives for abolition, suffrage, reform for prostitution and laws to raise the age of consent, as well as prohibition.

In 1913, the Women's Christian Temperance Union, with almost 250,000 members, inspired hundreds of members and other supporters to march on Washington, D.C.—just like many reform movements of today—demanding an amendment banning the sales of alcohol in the United States. Although they succeeded in law, they ultimately failed to change human hearts and behavior.

After the successful ratification of the Eighteenth Amendment to the U.S. Constitution in 1919, this social reform largely collapsed under the weight of its own consequences. The challenge to eliminate alcohol was complicated by loopholes in the law for pharmacies, the rise of organized crime, and the advent of the Great Depression. Simply put, the American people would not obey this law and the loss of revenue and jobs made lucrative efforts to flout the law too great. The Twenty-first Amendment repealed Prohibition in 1933.

Two speeches highlight this reform topic. "Everybody's War," from Frances E. Willard, the second president and life-time leader of the Women's Christian Temperance Union, the most successful women's group the nation had ever seen, is the first text. In it, she sets forth her arguments that alcohol is the source of all social ills. She portrays abstinence and prohibition as a holy war between the evil "rumsellers" and noble "churches" who preserve the social order of God, country and home. This effort Willard publicly billed for women reluctant to become involved in unladylike social causes as "Home Protection." This speech sets the stage for the reform movement that both embraced larger causes of domestic violence, voting rights, the needs of orphans, reforms for prostitution, and equality for women in its time, and is also instructive for the pressing social reforms of our time.

The second public address, "On Prohibition," is the simple remarks to a reporter given by controversial mega church pastor, faith healer, and celebrity evangelist, Aimee Semple McPherson before her 1930 trip to the Holy Land. This address was a public statement to the press when asked about her position on prohibition. Her wise—and witty—answer included a story about a preacher who wished to dump all forms of alcohol into the river and then called his congregation to sing the hymn "Shall We Gather at the River." Apparently, his error, to McPherson reflected the ambiguity of wanting to be good, yet acting like the flawed humanity we are.

Frances E. Willard (1839–1898)

Temperance is moderation in the things that are good and total abstinence
from the things that are foul.

—Motto of the Women's Christian Temperance Union

In many ways, Frances E. Willard was ahead of her time. She chose a
single life and became a community organizer, activist, and warrior
for social reforms. As President of the Woman's Christian Temperance
Union (WCTU) from 1879 to 1898, she was a champion in the cause of
prohibition, women's suffrage, and "social purity," an effort to raise
the age of consent and reform prostitution laws. A devout Christian,
Willard grounded her activism to addressing social ills for the better-
ment of a society hospitable for wives, children, and families. Women's
rights, including the vote, were necessary for the governance of the
home, an approach to feminist causes that might be unpopular today.

Raised in a Methodist family in Churchville, New York, Willard's
first career was in education as a teacher in eleven different schools,
and then as an administrator at the Women's College of Northwestern.
After some disagreements with the university's president, she resigned
and began a new career in the temperance movement.

Under her leadership as the second president of the WCTU, the
organization grew to become the largest women's organization in the
world at that time. The temperance movement's central focus was to
abolish the social ills caused by the sale of hard liquor. Some "crusad-
ers" would enter saloons and places where liquor was sold and try to
convince them to stop selling it. This reform movement recognized the
connection between drunkenness, prostitution, and poverty for families of alcoholic men. The moral superiority of women is a key theme
of Willard's rhetoric.

The address, "Everybody's War" was given in Chicago in 1874,
early in Willard's career with the WCTU. In it, Willard is addressing
the men, women, and children in her audience with the fiery rhetoric
of holy war. The speech is one of vivid imagery and contrasts, a war
between the good of the home, family, church, and country against the

evil of "rumsellers" and "saloons" that are the harbingers of moral ruin and decay. She appeals to the moral authority of women as wives and mothers to join the fight against the evils of alcohol.

The speech opens with the tale of a man who is speaking with a lady of the WCTU. He shows her a picture of himself as a young man full of promise contrasted with the dissolute man he has become through whiskey. He asks the woman to view the picture "for his mother's sake." Following this attempt to elicit sympathetic feelings for this victim of the drink, Willard calls for engagement in the holy war being waged against three societal foundations: God, country, and family.

First, the holy war against the forces of good sets up the contrast between the church and the saloon. She proclaims that the church is outnumbered and outgeneraled by the sheer numbers of bars versus the number of churches in Chicago. She compares a man's education with the lessons, music, and literature of the saloon with the education of Sunday School. One of the reformed men tells her that in the saloon, Christ is considered an "old wife's fable." Later, she asks her audience how God's will can be done, as the Lord's Prayer says, with the prosperity of the saloons?: "How is he going to rule until we get all the rum shops out of the way?"

Second, the patriot's war, declares Willard is waged against the America of the Pilgrim Fathers and William Penn by the merchants of alcohol. Willard avers that "such people" in other lands and times may accept public inebriation that we cannot accept in Christian America. [1] She also warns about the corruption that follows the choices of drunken voters.

The final war is that "of mothers and daughters, sisters and wives" who want to protect hearth and home. Willard appeals to mothers who do not have sons so that their daughters will not risk becoming "the drunkard's wife." She urges the husbands, sons, and fathers to remember the women when they cast their ballots.

Willard closes with the story of her little sister who died of typhoid as a child. In her recounting, the dying girl admonishes Willard to, "tell everybody to be good." It's the call that drives Willard, a voice calling for social reform so that everybody might do better, and in fact be good.

* * *

"Everybody's War" (1874)[2]

Clark Street Methodist Church

Chicago, Illinois

1874

At one of the meetings of the Woman's Temperance Union there was a poor fellow present, written all over from head to foot with evidence of a dissolute life. He came to the altar after the meeting and said to the speaker, "I want you to remain a few moments when the rest are gone for I have something I propose to show you."

Now boys and girls I want you to listen. What do you suppose it was? He took out of his pocket an old soiled package—he took off a paper and inside of that was another, a little cleaner. He took off and inside was another and inside of that was a tissue paper, nice and white, and inside of all this was a photograph. It represented a young man about eighteen years old, a pleasant, nice looking young fellow. She looked at this man who was standing before her, so distressed an object in every way, and she said curiously, this photograph represents a friend of yours perhaps, and what do you supposed he answered her? "Well lady, I ain't showed myself much of a friend to him. That photo is me, before I took myself to drinking whisky and I thought to show it to you for my mother's sake." She looked at the frank, open face of the photograph and at the bleared, sad, wrinkled face of the man; at the nice white collar and nice tie in the photograph, then at the thin collarless shirt of the man. Standing before her so weary and troubled, lay in his happy boyhood days sleeping upon his mother's breast. She thought of the time when first his footsteps wandered beyond the shelter of the great happy home towards the sinful resorts that we legalize on either side along our street. Then she turned to the man and photograph, and turned her eyes to heaven with that old cry, "How long, Oh God, how long?" [Ps. 13:1]

This sort of thing might do for others—for other lands, but it will not do for the land of the star spangled banner. It may have done for other times, but it will not do for the nineteenth century. It may do for other people, but it will not do for the descendants of the Pilgrim Fathers and William Penn.

I say there is a war about it in America. A war about that sort of thing which changes men so that their mothers after a few years would not know them, for though all mothers may not have their hearts broken—may have no sons—no boys who carried on to destruction, yet our Christian republic may not legalize the deadly traffic in that which they know by observation is likely in all cases to lead to that precise result.

Ladies of the north side, I am sad but frank to say it, there has not been so much interest shown in this quarter of the city as in others in the temperance movement by the women.

I want to ask you now, if you have not formed before in this work, hadn't you better in the name of these boys and girls sitting here. Hadn't you better? I came here to-day [sic] through blocks and blocks of saloons, and almost under the very shadow of great grinding distilleries. There are no insurance policies upon your homes. The rum shops have the free run of the whole place—the home of the American Eagle.

Remember it is simply a matter of fact that from the rum shops every year in America sixty thousand of our own citizens reel out inebriated and taste a drunkard's death. There are half a million steady drinkers, behind this a million moderate drinkers, behind them two million occasional drinkers, behind them all little boys go tramp, tramp, tramp to a drunkard's tomb. And remember these reinforcing ranks, for they are always full, you know, must be recruited from somebody's cradle, from somebody's fireside, perhaps your own, no matter how stately or proud your home may be. Some ladies say to me with all sobriety, saying it at the same time, "I wish the best in the world for your good cause—I hope it will succeed, but then I have no boys." Perhaps you have daughters and not sons. If you have not, somebody has and somebody has boys. If you have daughters and not sons, try to fathom the unfathomable lessons of these words, "*a drunkard's wife.*"

There is a war about this in America, a war of mothers and daughters, sisters and wives. There is another sort of war and I want to have the boys and girls follow me as I talk to them and I think I can make you understand me. There is a war between the rum shops and religion. They stand against each other, insurmountable and unassailable foes. You know that the late Willian F. Steward wrote of our late war as our irrepressible conflict. We have an irrepressible conflict, a war to the knife and the knife to the hilt. Only one can win, the question is which one is it going to be. Now think about it. In this war with them, I take it we Christians of the church, we outnumber them.

Did you ever think of it, little people? There are in this city, for instance, a number of churches and for every church there are from twenty-five to thirty whiskey shops. There are for every minister twenty-five to thirty barkeepers, and while the churches only meet and open their blessed door once or twice, or at the most four or five times a week, the whiskey shops grind on their mill of destruction all the weeks of every month, and all the months of every year.

We are outnumbered or are we not. We are outgeneraled by the people who keep the rum shops—we who keep the Sunday school and the church. They have a series of lessons, international if you please, with which ours of the Sunday school does not compare at all. They have their music of which I would not speak, their literature free by license of which I would not think. One of our reformed men was talking with me one day of a friend of his who had signed the pledge and broken it. He was discouraged. He had taken a binding pledge and broken it again and again. This is what the reformed man said to me. I said you don't understand this business, that is all. You are new in the business. You must not get discouraged. Don't give Tim up or anything of the sort! You remember he is a graduate in a seven years course in a saloon. It took him seven years to learn all that education in the saloon, now give him a year or two to unlearn it—the education of the saloon.

Then the man went on to say "do you know that, in the saloon, conscience is considered a fraud and a jest? Do you know that in the saloon the religion of Christ is considered just simply an old wife's fable? That Christ is an exploded myth, the Christ of whom you women like to talk about is only the fevered fancy of a woman's dreams?" I tell you my eyes have been opened with wonder to see things I didn't use[d] to see at all. I saw dead friends going up and down our streets. I saw things I liked to see. I saw pleasant homes on every side of the way. I saw churches which are suggestive of immortal hope. I saw bookstores at once honey hives of thought.

Do you know that until the Woman's Crusade came sweeping up over our prairies, I never cared. I never saw a saloon—it was a question with which I had nothing to do. It was nothing to me. I hoped it would succeed but I did not see it the same as I do today. Let me tell you young people the way I seem to see it now. You just reflect. I go up and down the streets here in Chicago. I go up and down the streets of other towns and cities throughout the west on the errand I believe God sent me to go upon. If I did not believe it I would not go. I see in one corner church spires, both stately and pointing heavenward. I see over on another corner of the same street a schoolhouse with doors opening wide—and little boys and girls, youths and maidens drinking at the pure fountain of knowledge. And between these two are institutions called a saloon, equally guaranteed by our laws—equally fostered by our nation; and more than equally patronized by our people. There is no boy or girl so high that they don't know what I mean. It has a sanded floor, its curtains half way down. It has a screen across the front so you can't see what is going on inside. It has fumes and odors coming out that makes you wish you had passed on the other side. You know I mean the rum shop.

Let us go in with this man who was taught at our Sunday schools. When he was the least bit of a boy he sat on his father's knee, Sunday after Sunday, with an honorable and useful life stretching before him when the minister spoke of life, duty and destiny and another life coming on afterwards. Let us go in with him, with this boy who later was taught in our public schools until he knew something of the world.

But he got in the way of going in here. He did not go at first because he wanted to but because someone asked him to. He did only as often as young men did, and he thought it the proper thing to do, to be sociable. As the habit grew upon him, he failed in business, his friends deserted him, he lost those who were dearer to him than life, then he did not care. Let us go in with some friend and see this transaction. Behind the counter stands avarice, before the counter appetite, and between the two a transaction that puts a few dimes into the till of the proprietor and throws voluntary insanity into the brain of the patron. The man goes out, he goes to the primary meeting and election, he loiters away his time, he fritters away his earnings. He goes to the house where he is best beloved, to the best friends he has in the world, where they love him better than they do anybody else. Yet upon that wife that loves him so well and little children clinging about his neck he inflicts atrocities which imagination cannot picture and no tongue dare describe.

Now I am not telling you anything that does not happen in Chicago a hundred times a day. If it had happened away up among the [Eskimos], if it had happened down among the South Sea Islanders, or on the prairies where the wild Indians live, we would say it is just what we should expect of such people. But these rum shops do exist and this rum traffic is going on by permission and apathy of well-born, well-bred and well-taught Americans. These rum shops exist in the shape of Juggernaut's old car. They stand in the shadow of the sacred wide arms of the cross of Christ, the Jesus Christ our Lord. That is why there is a war in America.

I shall not dwell long on that, but pass on to the taxpayers' revolt. We the people don't see the effect of all this. You know, we used to say we must have this money to help pay the taxes, this liquor tax of seventy millions a year. But we have found out that the liquor traffic makes a cat's paw out of the taxpayers to rake in the hot chestnuts of ninety millions a year for extra paraphernalia. I want the boys particularly to remember this—that more than all the revenues derived from the whiskey shops must go to build prisons, must go to the hospital, the home for the friendless, police justices and police officers to take care of these people who go crazy on purpose and to pay for all that so it costs us yearly the difference between seventy and ninety millions of dollars. Twenty millions lost. I want you to think about that.

Another thing—I don't suppose everybody who is listening to me knows what all these drinks are made of. Out of nice clean grain that grows out of the ground, wheat, rye, barley, corn. We use in America forty millions of bushels of nice clean grain that turned over into alcoholic drinks every year. Now a good man has found out by mathematical calculation that we drink enough to pay for paving a good wide street all the way from Chicago to New York. The yearly drink bill in Illinois is forty-two millions of dollars and in the country six hundred millions. There is no use in stopping to dwell longer upon these statistics. These are facts and figures which we cannot deny. We have to take this money out of our pockets and pay it to the very last cent. This we find out from Secretary [of the Treasury] Bristow in his last report—so it is plain enough.

There is another kind of war—it is a patriot's war. I do not believe there is one boy or girl here to-night that he or she does not revere the old flag, the red, white and blue. I remember when I was a little girl, away up in Wisconsin, the 4th of July. I remember when we had our little procession and flag made from a pillow case with red calico stripes sewed on and gold stars pinned on the corner. I was going to talk about the harm the liquor traffic does to the country and the flag we love so well, for I tell you I always loved the flag.

Yes, it is a patriot's war because in our country we get up public opinion. Everybody thinks one man's vote is as good as another, even though he staggers up to the polls and drops in the ballot on election day. Our people are made to think you cannot change the habits and drinking customs they had across the sea where one man is not as good as another on election day, where they have such a different government altogether. We should I think remember what difference there is between them and us. We are taught to pray, "Thy kingdom come, thy will be done" where? "On earth." We sing in the sacred hymn, "bring forth the diadem and crown him Lord of all." We as people believe what this good book says when it plainly again and again declares that Christ is again going to rule on earth. How is he going to rule until we get all the rum shops out of the way?

Now let us take the contrast—there is Germany, let us take that. Germany is a country governed by a hereditary monarch. They know who is to be the next king. This king, he rules until he is relieved by death.

Then his son rules and so on in the never ending formulae. They never ask who is going to be the next President, they know who is going to be the next king. In America, every man is King—King over whom? King over his own self. In Germany, they are ruled by two million bayonets. In America, ballots are bayonets. Every drunkard and every rumseller holds that in his hand, which may shake the very President in his chair. In America there are one million drunkards and rumsellers who stagger up to the polls and exercise that sacred right. They are in every ward, in every precinct and every election district. They stagger up to the polls and drop their bleared ballots. What fruits can we expect by salary grabbers, credit rings, whiskey rings, post tradership ring, and every sort except the ring of true metal.

Going on at this rate no one needs to be a prophet to see what this thing will lead to. It is a patriot's war indeed, it is everybody's war, great and small, from the least to the greatest, and what a war it is. We must guard it as we would a foreign foe. I like the idea of marching along with men and women who have their eyes open. I like to go along keeping time to the same music, even singing that good old song, "I'm glad I'm in this army / I will battle for the cause." You think maybe the crusade is dead and its banner is trailing in the dust. I tell you no. The women who marched with the crusade—don't you believe they are somewhere? The children of these men and women are being sworn at the home altars against this traffic as Hannibal was sworn against Rome. The method has changed, but the movement is just the same. If the world was asleep, you young people would understand that, but the world is awake; its heart is sad, its lips are apart, and its eyelids wide.

I am here tonight, dear friends, an American woman forever grateful to the land that has been so good to me and whose path in life has been turned out of the expected channel by the crusade. I am here to ask you just this simple question. Is all this anything at all to you? How do you stand [a]ffected by it? How are you toward the temperance reform? How are you in the sentiments you cherish in your hearts, that is it. You know what Mrs. [Harriet Beecher] Stowe said about it. If you can't say anything about it, you can feel right. How are you in the sentiments you express? How are you on election day, when aldermen are to be elected? How are you when a notice comes for a primary? How do you stand on the question of New Year's Day? How do you stand in the social sanctity? Let me tell you it makes all the difference in the world how you stand, though you never say one word or give one dollar toward our cause. If you only just care.

There is a noble fellow on the board of trade in this city who said to me the other day—I can't do much for the cause. I read about it and think about it but it has just come into my head what I could do. I often am asked when closing a bargain to go out and take a glass of beer or even something stronger. I always used to and used to say to them, "I don't care" and thought it was the proper thing to do. I just stopped short off—I will not do it. When men ask me I will say I have joined the temperance ranks—I believe as the women do. That man is a walking temperance lecturer, better than nine-tenths of the temperance lecturers, for he acts.

I think we are all sympathetic on this subject. I don't believe there is any difference between us in the contest. We are moving on the enemy's track. I think if I were to ask any little boy or girl here the reason why these people carry on this business, the answer would be because there is money in it. That goes straight to the mark. That answer is exactly right. There is this about it, there are large sums of money invested in this traffic. Ours is no light reform. There is seven hundred millions invested in this rum traffic this very day, and you know the way to get at these men is to touch them in their pocketbooks. Every man who is reformed by our efforts makes that much less revenue for them. This seven hundred millions ought to be taken out of this rum traffic and be invested in other branches of trade which would go toward making up our national life and prosperity.

I want to say a few more words more before I close. I want to say just this one thing more on this subject. In a few days from now you will be called upon to go to the polls in as much as there are to be thirty-six or thirty-eight aldermen to be elected in the city of Chicago. It is a vital question to us what sort of men they are. Although the women cannot go to the polls to vote, let me urge upon their sons and husbands here.

Will you remember, good sirs, that when you go to the election you represent more than you did once. You represent more thoughts, more work, more prayers. Remember whom you want and whom you will have.

Let us work and pray for the good time coming when this city shall be redeemed. Although we are not voters, we are daughters of America as much as you are sons and patriots. We need money to carry on this war. We cannot like King Midas turn everything into gold. I know that times are hard. You have your office rents to pay and all your other expenses, but we need money to buy temperance literature and different things we have to carry on this war. And when you can give a dollar, remember that you cannot give it to a more worthy cause than ours.

And often to me nowadays comes the thought of something in my life very dear and distant—something which I do not hesitate to speak to you about. I want to speak to you about my sister, loved and lost. Many years ago away up in Wisconsin where we spend our girlhood days—that girl was my only playmate, and there upon a fallen tree trunk Little Lizzie, she would stand and make a temperance speech to me, little thing, and I in turn would make one to her just for play. And now I think as I go about this new and strange work that she knows about it, that I am not alone.

I am reminded of the sad, sweet message she left when she went away from us. It was on a bright June morning when she died and Father said to her, for he loved her, no one better than her, "My child, if I should tell you that God wanted you, how would you feel?" She turned to him almost reproachfully and said, "Father, I did not think I should die because you know I am so young. And yet if God should want me I would say take me home." She said—"It is Christ I want, I wish he would come nearer." Although I never had prayed before, Father and Mother and I knelt beside her dying and we prayed that she might feel the grasp of Father's hand, so kind and loving. I remember she smiled, and said, "Sister, you need not pray now, he has come. It seems as if he is all my own." And then she [lay] her dying head upon the pillow and looked at me with that strange look in her eyes which were growing dim. She uttered these last words, "Sister, I want you to tell everybody to be good." Then she turned her face away and when I saw it next it had upon it that smile of God's eternal peace.

I say to-night I want to leave in your hearts these burning words. I do not think I shall ever forget her sweet dying message. I wish it might be remembered as she so greatly expressed it, "be good." Be good and help everybody to be good who needs help. God grant that each of us this night may have a clear formula of life which should be nothing more or less than be good.

Aimee Semple McPherson (1890–1944)

"I pledged to Him my all, if He would take me, unworthy though I was, empty me of self and make me...a vessel through which His own Message might flow."[3]

By any standard, Aimee Semple McPherson was a "rock star" among women of religious faith. On the one hand, from humble beginnings, she became pastor and founder of Los Angeles' Angelus Temple, the first American megachurch drawing thousands of believers and tourists alike; she also founded the denomination, The Foursquare Church (Jesus as Savior, Baptizer, Healer, and Coming King). An international celebrity of the 1920s, McPherson was known for her faith healing, theatrical religious services, entrepreneurial acumen with the press, and public personae mixing celebrity and biblical piety. In every way, she was a Christian star in the roaring twenties. She managed to proclaim her message across the nation, as a single mom with two young children, at a time when women were not even permitted to vote.

On the other hand, she was also the focus of scandal and scorn from minsters who felt threatened by her success with common people, her three marriages, extravagant spending, and public family disputes. Critics also debated her May 1926 five-day disappearance and alleged abduction with the account of others who testified about a possible adulterous tryst. Even as times changed and her influence waned, McPherson was a force to be reckoned with.

This brief public address is included in this section as a coda to Frances Willard's speech on prohibition, as McPherson is leaving on a trip to the Holy Land just before Easter. In it, the "reform" presented is the very life of Aimee Semple McPherson, as a woman who defied every duty of normal convention. Ignoring her critics for the call of God on her life, "Sister Aimee" gave a slightly different reading about prohibition as a social reform. She told the story of a man who preached his desire to throw all alcohol in the river and then later invited the congregation to sing, "Shall We Gather at the River?" McPherson recognized the contradiction of human nature to aspire to higher ideals while failing to live a fully virtuous life in the real world. This may be her appeal and legacy as people of faith seek to create a better world today, while acknowledging human limitations.

* * *

"On Prohibition" (1930)[4]

Los Angeles, CA

1930

Leaving Los Angeles for New York, and the boat, upon which we sail immediately, I was met en route by multitudes of our friends. Among them ever was a liberal sprinkling of newspaper men. And in each city, they asked the same question: "Sister McPherson, what do you think of Prohibition?"

It was rather difficult to answer the question in such a few words as one must use then, but I told them, that the case about Prohibition here in the United States, reminds me of the story of the lecturer who gave a marvelous address on Prohibition. And he wound up in a blaze of glory that brought everyone to their feet enthusiastically: "Why is it my friends, if I had my way, do you know what I'd do? I'd take every barrel of liquor, every bottle of booze, every crate, and I'd empty it in the river. Yes, sir." Then he said, "Shall we now close our meeting by rising and singing, 'Shall We Gather at the River?'"

He'd spoiled it all. And that's the way perhaps with us over here in America: we teach it, but so often those who profess to make the laws do not quite live up to them, and back them themselves.

I wish that you could all have the joy of going with us this Easter tide to the Holy Land, where we shall visit on Easter Day, the tomb of our risen Lord.

Notes

1 Her bigotry and ethnocentrism are disturbing to the modern reader and reflect the attitudes of her place and time.

2 Richard W. Leeman, *"Do Everything" Reform: The Oratory of Frances E. Willard* (Westport, CT: Greenwood Press, 1992), 111–119. Words that Leeman found "undecipherable" are replaced with words from the edited transcript in: Carolyn De Swarte Gifford and Amy R. Slagell, eds. *Let Something Good Be Said: Speeches and Writings of Frances E. Willard* (Chicago, IL: University of Chicago Press, 2007), 1–9.

3 Aimee Semple McPherson, *Fire From on High*, "Preface" (Los Angeles, CA Foursquare Publications, 1969), 3.

4 Aimee Semple McPherson, "On Prohibition" (speech, Los Angeles, CA, 1930), YouTube video, 1:31, posted by "Rev Donald Spitz BabyCakesDavid," March 15, 2009, https://www.youtube.com/watch?v=U0bXH1YgKf4, accessed March 31, 2018. Authenticity certified as this text was transcribed from audio from YouTube video.

Human Freedom

Slavery is a wasting disease in the body politic of every human civilization. No matter how well a slaveowner treats his or her slaves, the very idea of owning another person is repugnant. Human freedom and ability to choose how one will live is the cure for the disordered thinking that supports the enslavement of others. Unfortunately, the rhetoric of religion has often upheld slavery in the United States. And, religion has inspired many to fight for abolition and freedom. From Wilber Wilberforce and the Clapham Circle of religious reformers who helped abolish Great Britain's slave trade in 1807 to activists seeking to stop today's human trafficking, the call to faith resounds in the duty of believers to bring their neighbors out of bondage.

Many early reformers in the United States were first wave feminists, who connected freedom from slavery to the rights of women. The first speaker, Sojourner Truth was a stalwart voice for blacks and women, and she continues to inspire long after her death in 1883. For Truth, the facts of her message, "Ain't I a Woman?," include the witness of her own life. Her Christian faith permeates her address as she challenges those who oppose women's rights, and African American women's rights, when she says, "Where did your Christ come from? From God and a woman! Man had nothing to do with him." Truth lived as a slave and then as a free woman. While uneducated, her natural rhetorical skill and quick mind challenged the belief that women were inferior and needed protection. She admonishes the white men in the audience to let the women "to get it right up side again."

Dr. Brook Bello is the second speaker who grounds her message in the witness of her own life overcoming abduction and trafficking to become a successful businesswoman, writer, actor, and advocate through her faith in God. In "The Beautiful Color of Freedom," Bello urges her audience to "come up higher" and not grow weary in the task of letting victims of trafficking and abuse know that "it is not their fault." As an ordained minister, CEO, and founder of the non-profit More Too Life, Bello has an impressive track record of influence. She has appeared on platforms with presidents, other legislators, and community leaders, while also implementing practical programs to help young people, women, and men to find a better life. Dr. Bello has also helped enact legislation to help decriminalize child prostitution and created court-sanctioned programming for men to help them understand the impact of exploitation on women's lives.

Both speakers argue for human freedom from their Christian faith and the veracity of their own stories to serve as living parables of transformation. These rhetors each have lived the consequences of their messages and the relevance of their claims. Their lives communicate the transcendent value of freedom and equality through their belief in God and call to advocate and serve others. Their speeches and activism stand as witness to the duty of involvement and the destiny of human dignity.

Sojourner Truth (1797–1883)

If my cup won't hold but a pint, and yours holds a quart, wouldn't you be
mean not to let me have my little half measure full?

Born Isabella (Belle) Baumfree as a slave in 1797, Sojourner Truth became
a powerful abolitionist, preacher, and advocate for African American
and women's rights. Moreover, she physically symbolized strong womanhood in her lifetime, standing six feet tall, and having a deep, low
speaking voice and beautiful singing voice—all contributing to her ethos
and delivery. She spoke with plain-spoken power of her experiences as
an abused slave and manual laborer. This speech, "Ain't I a Woman?,"
is her most remembered public address. Given in Akron, Ohio, at the
Women's Rights Convention, May 28, 1851, this speech was given to a
mixed gender audience that included several ministers. One minister
in attendance had argued that if God had wanted women to be equal
with men, it would have been evident from the "birth, life and death" of
Christ; another said that Eve's sin determined women's inferior station.[1]
With a podium so full of educated, polished speakers advocating wom-
en's rights, having Truth speak was controversial indeed.

Her few words, however, spoke volumes. To the argument that
women are delicate and "need to be helped into carriages," Truth proclaimed, "Look at me! Look at my arm! I have ploughed and planted,
and gathered into barns, and no man could head me! Ain't I a woman?"
She argued that she not only did the work of a man, but she faced the
lash of slavery as well. To the minister who argued that Christ was
male, she answered, "Where did your Christ come from? From God
and a woman. Man had nothing to do with Him." Truth's bold, direct
style got the undivided attention of the convention. According to Frances Gage, the woman who presided over the meeting, "I have never
in my life seen anything like the magical influence that subdued the
mobbish spirit of the day and turned the jibes and sneers of the crowd
into notes of respect and admiration."[2]

* * *

"Ain't I a Woman?" (1851)[3]

Women's Rights Convention

Akron, Ohio

1851

Well, children, where there is so much racket there must be something out of kilter. I think that 'twixt the negroes of the South and the women at the North, all talking about rights, the white men will be in a fix pretty soon. But what's all this here talking about?

That man over there says that women need to be helped into carriages, and lifted over ditches, and to have the best place everywhere. Nobody ever helps me into carriages, or over mud-puddles, or gives me any best place! And ain't I a woman? Look at me! Look at my arm! I have ploughed and planted, and gathered into barns, and no man could head me! And ain't I a woman? I could work as much and eat as much as a man—when I could get it—and bear the lash as well! And ain't I a woman? I have borne thirteen children, and seen most all sold off to slavery, and when I cried out with my mother's grief, none but Jesus heard me! And ain't I a woman?

Then they talk about this thing in the head; what's this they call it? [member of audience whispers, "intellect"] That's it, honey. What's that got to do with women's rights or negroes' rights? If my cup won't hold but a pint, and yours holds a quart, wouldn't you be mean not to let me have my little half measure full?

Then that little man in black there, he says women can't have as much rights as men, 'cause Christ wasn't a woman! Where did your Christ come from? Where did your Christ come from? From God and a woman! Man had nothing to do with Him.

If the first woman God ever made was strong enough to turn the world upside down all alone, these women together ought to be able to turn it back, and get it right side up again! And now they is asking to do it, the men better let them.

Obliged to you for hearing me, and now old Sojourner ain't got nothing more to say.

Dr. Brook Bello

"Victim to survivor, survivor to thriver, thriver to champion."

Dr. Brook Bello is a real hero. The motto of More Too Life, the organization she founded is, "Victim to survivor, survivor to thriver, thriver to champion."[4] Bello passionately fights the battle against human trafficking and embodies the inspiring truth of overcoming the hardships of abuse to become a champion of social justice and culture change as an advocate for women and children worldwide. In 2016, she was honored as part of the United Way Worldwide series, "The Hero Effect," aired on the Oprah Winfrey Network (OWN), for her tireless work as a human rights activist. In addition, President Obama awarded Dr. Bello with the Lifetime Achievement Award in 2016. Also, Florida's Attorney General Pam Bondi and Governor Rick Scott named her Advocate of the Year in 2017. She was also named a Next Gen Google Policy Leader in 2018.

As she testified to the Florida Legislature when endorsing a bill to change wording in the laws (HB369 and HB465), Dr. Bello described her own experience. After being raped at age eleven, she said, "I was taken to a dirty hotel room, beaten up, injected with drugs, and that became my life for several years." Her testimony influenced the language in these bills to exclude the idea that children can be prostitutes. These bills were overwhelmingly voted into law. This is only one example of Bello's life changing work as a speaker and leader alongside presidents, legislators, and community activists.

From her story, Dr. Bello has achieved career success as a film maker, actor, author, and international leader and speaker. She is also an ordained minister and chaplain with a passion for exposing the underlying causes of human trafficking and sexual violence, through her positive message of hope in God and the inherent worth of every human being. Her court-approved program for men, Restorative Justice End Demand Education (RJEDE), helps participants understand the causes and consequences of sexual exploitation and modern-day slavery.

With the creation of "Living Above The Noise" (LATN), a mentoring and identity discovery education curriculum, Dr. Bello aims to educate and inspire young victims on how to overcome the idea that any kind of victimization was their fault, and teach them how to live a life beyond the trauma. This curriculum encompasses internet safety, healthy relationships and lifestyles, budgeting classes, and many other skills needed to be successful and proactive in life.

Dr. Bello shared this address, "The Beautiful Color of Freedom," at the More Too Life Legacy Festival in Sarasota, Florida's Newtown neighborhood, February 2015, during African American Heritage Month. She shares her story and calls her audience to "come up higher" into the life of dignity God has for them. The transcendent value of human freedom rings true in her own story and struggle as she calls her hearers to "rise up," cherish and advocate for the innocence of children and for teens who never even knew what innocence was.

Dr. Bello urges her audience to shake off the bonds of indifference. Making use of biblical journey images, such as "cross over" and "come higher," Dr. Bello urges her listeners to recognize and heal the wounds of abused women and those who have fallen through the cracks. Realizing that their abuse "was never their fault," by faith, each victim can rise up, and embrace the dignity and "best life" God has to offer. Through her witness and Christian action, Dr. Bello is living proof and the finest argument of her empowering message.

The facts of her message include a wake-up call for her listeners to help victims know of their victimization, popular culture's influence on the trivialization of young girl's innocence, and the restoration of persons who have fallen through society's cracks. The consequences include a choice between a mediocre life or a life of divine destiny. She admonishes her audience to get ever closer to intervening with a child, a mother, and father, or a family, through faith in God. Her warrant to this call is the witness to her own life. The transcendent value is human freedom, restored families, and a reach to not giving up on the neighbors God calls us to love.

* * *

"The Beautiful Color of Freedom" (2015)[5]

More Too Life Legacy Festival

Sarasota, Florida

February 28, 2015

Harriet Tubman said, "I have freed one thousand slaves, and I could have freed one thousand more if they only knew they were slaves." Do we? Victims don't know they don't know they are victims; will you tell them they are victims? Come up higher, come up higher to the place of clarity in your mind and be free. The great ball women said, "Oh while I live to be the ruler of life not a slave to meet light as a powerful conquer and nothing experiencing me will ever take command of me." We must not allow the things on the outside to take command of our heart and our mind. For us, this means pop culture norms. Eighty percent of all we learn—babies listen to me—eighty percent of all we learn is based is on the images we see. What do you see in your heart on TV, and all around you and how will you counteract those negative images with images of power, of beauty and destiny, and build life, and dare to dream?

For God has said, as he laid face to face through the eyes of Christ, "with man, it is impossible with God, all things are possible." We look past the non-lyrical ills of some of today's hip hop and so-called R&B and rock music that speaks of the killing of one another, the degradation of family and girls, and even little boys, and we bounce to it, like motion for bouncing to as though it is rhythmic beauty and harmonious power. And we sway back and forth, and women and reach will we come up higher to a place of promise and innocence? Will little girl's virginity still be stolen away killing the soul and heart of the beauty of being washed in the love and virginity and stillness of what it really means to simply be a kid again.

When is the last time you ever saw a kid "Skip-to-my-Lou-my-Darling"? Skip to soft music and the simple pleasures of butterflies, birds, bees and flowers? When you respect that justice, and just because a thirteen-year-old girl says yes to a twenty plus or older man for sex that groomed her sweet innocent self, with too much for her fatherless self or a damn it so much coming from an unhealed mother in need or a broken home, does not mean she wanted it. As the statutory rape law in the state of Florida and around the world is there to protect her for that reason, who will you protect today.

Where do we go from here when many have misunderstood or become too tired to fight for the rights of the innocent more and when younger people don't even know what innocence is. Where do we go from here? Pain will subside, but if you quit reaching for all that is good in your life, you will never know. Take this challenge with us today, take the challenge because we double dare you, I double dare you, to step from pain to promise and from the proclivities and disparities of life, by faith to in a light shining forth. Listen well. Who God has tested you to be right, rise up from where you are now. Can you see in the future? If not, you will remain in mediocrity and you will never taste the full mouth or the success that only bears your name.

There are 168 hours per week for everyone rich or poor, black or white. What will you do with yours? I have come from hell of suicidal thoughts of despair, drug addiction to live a life of promise and by faith as an actress, an author, and filmmaker, and then an ordained minister crawling up out of the holes and hell holes that God pulled me out, and God is still not finished with me yet. For many young people, and those who slip through the cracks, must understood that they too can reach higher. Even women who look grown, who slipped through the cracks when it wasn't called modern day human trafficking, more violated and have grown and don't really understand that they were victims and it was never their fault. What will we do across every jurisdictional line, demographic line, color line, to touch the life of someone else.

When God places something in you He ignites by His Holy Spirit so that you could not do in the natural on your own laurels or strength, you can do this in his wisdom. He touches it so that it is supernatural in you. The scripture says and the exceeding greatness of his power to us who believe according to the working of his mighty strength in us. Where do we go from here? What is freedom to you, and will you walk in the audacity to be great to tread though the money and ill-will waters of depression and marginalism to soar beyond great height into your destiny now today. This day. February 28th, 2015, in the year of our Lord. Call attention to yourself, search your own hearts, live for the best God has for you, but you might be an answer to the problem and there is no place great you won't go. Come up higher.

There is more to life; there is more to your life.

Cross over into the new wineskin, higher to a place where your dreams ignite and fire a bright luminous wonder every closer to the sunbeam of light,

Ever closer to saving the life of a child,

Ever closer to healing the life of an elder, ever ready to see your mother smile again and your father to stand tall and show up.

Come up higher, come up higher and greatness and the success of ending the abuse on children, on little black boys and girls, and white boys and white girls, and Latin girls and Latin boys. Come up higher, and the souls of women undone, the hearts of men will be done and mended. Fathers, can you hear me?

And in the tone of the great scripture, it will be, will be, said well done my good and faithful servant, well done for you have done all I have called you to do. Well done my good and faithful loved one. Well done! Hallelujah to his name! Hallelujah to his name! God bless you guys. God bless you. I am a miracle standing before you. The fact that I can even speak and delineate with no skepticism, but clarity who I am and who I will be; it's a miracle because once upon a time, my mind was not right to even speak before anyone, in any type of clarity. It is more than an ocean, so do not give up on your children, do not give up on your teens who seem lost, do not give up, and if you think you are all that, then obviously you need to come up higher and give. Love thy neighbor as thyself and you will have come up higher.

Notes

1   Olive Gilbert, *Narrative of Sojourner Truth: A Bondswoman of Olden Time* (Chicago, IL: Johnson Publishing Company, 1970), 104.

2 Ibid., 106.

3 Sojourner Truth, "Ain't I A Woman?" (speech, Women's Convention, Akron, OH, May 28, 1851), Infoplease (Sandbox Networks, Inc), accessed March 1, 2018, https://www.infoplease.com/us/speeches-primary-documents/aint-i-woman

4 Dr. Brook Bello, More Too Life or Youthiasm Inc, accessed March 1, 2018, https://moretoolife.org/

5 Dr. Brook Bello, "The Beautiful Color of Freedom" (speech, More Too Life Legacy Festival, Sarasota, FL, February 2015), YouTube video, 10:24, posted by "Brook Bello Inspires," May 4, 2015, https://www.youtube.com/watch?v=QPRNvOse-vOY Authenticity certified as this text was transcribed from audio from YouTube video.

Peacemaking

"Blessed are the peacemakers: for they shall be called the children of God."
— Jesus (Matthew 5:9, KJV)

How can we find peace in this broken world? The Hebrew concept of Shalom or wholeness of life, speaks to the universal longing for an end to war and the freedom to live in community, raise children, work, feed our families, get an education, and live a fruitful, healthy life. The elusive quest dances between the paradox of human desire for perfection and the real nature of human lust for power at the expense of others. In this section, we explore the speech texts of three women who were people of faith, public leaders in their contexts, and advocates for peace. In very different ways, they propose their visions for peacemaking and outline their duty to this cause.

These speeches share the transcendent value of the importance of human life. The messages vary with the speaker. One claims that abortion is the central cause of violence. Another avers that Christ calls for pacifism and against all forms of war. The final speaker refers to the importance of human kindness in the face of suffering as a way forward. While their approaches may differ, all three speakers have dedicated their lives to stand against human poverty and oppression. Once again, these speakers' lives and actions support the coherence and fidelity of their narratives. While controversial, their speeches reflect their religious values.

Mother Teresa is known for many things: her charitable work with the Missionaries of Charity, her inspirational work in the slums of Calcutta, her devotion to her Catholic faith, and her detractors who challenged her motives and ministry. In her speech to the National Prayer Breakfast, she challenges lawmakers and people of faith that abortion is the greatest destroyer of peace. President Bill Clinton and First Lady Hillary Clinton were in the audience that heard her that day.

Dorothy Day, also a devoted and controversial Roman Catholic, was famous for her work in the Catholic Worker Movement, which included houses of hospitality. This brief address, "Union Square Speech," speaks up for five young men who burned their draft cards during the Vietnam War. Her Catholic pacifism and deep dedication to the poor speak of her vision for peace.

The living leader of the Burmese people, Aung San Suu Kyi is affectionately known as "The Lady" to her people. Her life-long efforts to bring greater freedom to Myanmar (Burma), including denial of her election to parliament by the military, and later twelve-year house arrest, led the Nobel Committee to grant her the Nobel Peace Prize in 1991. Finally, in 2012, she was able to give her acceptance speech calling for greater peace and the practice of kindness, as inspired by her Buddhist religion.

Saint Mother Teresa (1910–1997)

"By blood, I am Albanian. By citizenship, an Indian. By faith, I am a Catholic nun. As to my calling, I belong to the world. As to my heart, I belong entirely to the Heart of Jesus."[1]

Mother Teresa—or Saint Teresa of Calcutta—was a complicated person who left an extraordinary legacy. On the one hand, she founded the Missionaries of Charity order in 1950 to serve the poorest of the poor. The

Missionaries of Charity now has more than 4,500 members serving in schools, soup kitchens, medical clinics, and places of dignity for dying people in more than 100 countries. Mother Teresa has inspired millions through her service, example, writing, and leadership. Her work with the terminally ill of Calcutta, India, is legendary. She is an international symbol of calling truth to power, speaking out of her devotion to Jesus Christ, and unwavering beliefs in the evil of abortion, divorce, and contraception. British journalist Malcolm Muggeridge noted, "Mother Teresa is fond of saying that welfare is for a purpose...whereas Christian love is for a person." [2] Teresa's canonization in 2016 confirms the enormous moral influence she holds among Roman Catholics, as well as people from other religions or no religion.

On the other hand, Mother Teresa and her mission had many critics. She has been accused of spiritually justifying terrible medical conditions in the houses of the dying, denying her patients pain medication that could lessen their suffering, as well as wasting the millions of dollars donated to the Missionaries of Charity. In addition, critics accuse her of caring more for conversion to Catholicism than bettering the lives of those who suffer, secret baptisms of those of other religions, and for her dogmatic stance on abortion, contraception, and divorce. [3]

In this 1994 speech to the National Prayer Breakfast in Washington, D.C., given before U.S. government representatives (including pro-choice President Bill Clinton, First Lady Hillary Clinton, Vice President Al Gore, and Mrs. Tipper Gore) and religious leaders. Mother Teresa's speech exemplifies the convictions and contradictions of her supporters and critics.

Mother Teresa opens her address to the 3,000 people who attended with prayer. She asks "where does love begin? Within our own families." After the crowd recites the Prayer of St. Francis together, Mother Teresa speaks simply about how Jesus Christ sacrificed himself to show God's love to the world, and how we are called to love one another by this sacrifice. She speaks about how Christ came to die "for you and me, and for the leper, the man over there dying of hunger." She compares Christ's thirst to the thirst of the elderly wanting to be wanted.

And then the speaker takes a politically-charged turn: "The greatest destroyer of peace today is abortion."

"If we accept that a mother can kill her unborn child," she asks her listeners, "then how can we tell other people not to kill one another?" She calls for mothers and fathers to "give until it hurts" and to receive a child as one would receive Jesus. Teresa speaks delightedly about the blessing her communities enjoy with adoption but says that she could not give a couple who had practiced contraception a child to adopt "for if a mother has destroyed the power of loving, how will she love my child?"

Mother Teresa extols the virtue of the poor to love and be spiritually rich while materially poor. Her example of a Hindu mother giving donated food to another family instead of to her own starving children as an act of love is troubling; it raises ethical questions about her claim that "the future of humanity passes through the family." While she received a standing ovation at the end, the Clintons and Gores remained silent.

* * *

"National Prayer Breakfast Address" (1994)[4]

Washington, D.C.

November 3, 1994

Make us worthy, Lord, to serve our fellow man throughout the world who live and die in poverty and hunger. Give them through our hands this day their daily bread, and by our understanding love, give peace and joy.

Jesus came to give us the good news that God loves us, and that He wants us to love one another as he loves each one of us. And to make it easy for us to love one another, Jesus said, "Whatever you do to the least, you do it to me." [Matt 25:40] "If you give a glass of water, you give it to me." [Matt 10:42]

And where does this love begin? In our own family.

How does it begin? By praying together.

Family that prays together, stays together. And if you stay together, you will love each other as God loves each one of you. So teach your children to pray, and pray with them; and you will have the joy and the peace and the unity of Christ's own love living in you.

As we have gathered together here, I think it will be beautiful if you begin with a prayer that expresses very well what Jesus wants us to do for the least. St. Francis of Assisi understood very well these words of Jesus and in his life very well expressed by prayer. And this prayer, which we say every day after Holy Communion, always surprises me very much, because it is very fitting for each one of us. And [I] always wonder whether 800 years ago, when St. Francis lived, they had the same difficulties that we have today. I think that some of you already have this prayer of peace, so we will pray it together.

Let us pray.

"Lord, make me a channel of your peace"—

Do you have the prayer book?

We will say it together?

"Lord, make me a channel of your peace,

where there is hatred, let me sow love;

where there is injury, pardon;

where there is doubt, faith;

where there is despair, hope;

where there is darkness, light;

where there is sadness, joy.

O, Divine Master, grant that I may Lord, grant that I may not so much seek to be consoled as to console;

to be understood as to understand;

to be loved as to love;

For it is in giving that we receive;

it is in pardoning that we are pardoned;

it is in dying that we are born again to Eternal Life."

Let us thank God for the opportunity He has given us today to have come here to pray together. We have come here especially to pray for peace, for joy, and for love. We are reminded that Jesus came to bring the good news to the poor. He had told us what is that good news when He said: "My peace I leave with you, My peace I give unto you" [John 14:27]. He came not to give the peace of the world, which is only that we don't bother each other. He came to give the peace of heart which comes from loving, from doing good to others.

And God loved the world so much that He gave His Son—it was a giving. God gave His son to the Virgin Mary, and what did she do with Him? As soon as Jesus came into Mary's life, immediately she went in haste to give that good news. And as she came into the house of her cousin, Elizabeth, Scripture tells us that the unborn child—the child in the womb of Elizabeth—leapt with joy. While still in the womb of Mary, Jesus brought peace to John the Baptist who leapt for joy in the womb of Elizabeth. The unborn was the first one to proclaim the coming of Christ.

And as if that were not enough, as if it were not enough that God the Son should become one of us and bring peace and joy while still in the womb of Mary, Jesus also died on the Cross to show that greater love. He died for you and for me, and for that leper, and for that man dying of hunger, and that naked person lying in the street, not only of Calcutta, but of Africa, and all over the world.

Our Sisters serve these poor people in 105 countries throughout the world. Jesus insisted that we love one another as He loves each one of us. Jesus gave His life to love us and He tells us that we also have to give whatever it takes to do good to one another. And in the Gospel Jesus says very clearly: "Love as I have loved you" [John 13:34].

Jesus died on the Cross because that is what it took for Him to do good to us—to save us from our selfishness and sin. He gave up everything to do the Father's will, to show us that we too must will-ing—must be willing to give up everything to do God's will—to love one another as He loves each one of us.

If we are not willing to give whatever it takes to do good to one another, sin is still in us. That is why we too must give to each other until it hurts. It is not enough to say—for us to say: "I love God." But I also have to love my neighbor. St. John says that you are a liar if you say you love God and you don't love your neighbor. How can you love God whom you do not see, if you do not love your neighbor whom you see, [1 John 4:20] whom you touch, with whom you live? And so it is very important for us to realize that love, to be true, has to hurt. I must be willing to give whatever it takes not to harm other people and, in fact, to do good to them. This requires that I be willing to give until it hurts. Otherwise, there is no true love in me; and I bring injustice, not peace, to those around me.

It hurt Jesus to love us. We have been created in His image for greater things, to love and to be loved. We must "put on Christ," as Scripture tells us. And so, we have been created to love as He loves us. Jesus makes Himself the hungry one, the naked one, the homeless one, the unwanted one, and He says, "You did it to Me." On the last day He will say to those on His right, "Whatever you did to the least of these, you did to Me." And He will also say to those on His left, "Whatever you neglected to do for the least of these, you neglected to do it for Me." When He was dying on the Cross, Jesus said, "I thirst." Jesus is thirsting for our love, and this is the thirst of everyone, poor and rich alike. We all thirst for love of others, that they go out of their way to avoid harming us and to do good to us. This is the meaning of true love, to give until it hurts.

I can never forget the experience I had in visiting a home where they kept all these old parents of sons and daughters who had just put them into an institution and forgotten them. Maybe. I saw that in that home these old people had everything—good food, comfortable place, television, everything, but everyone was looking toward the door. And I did not see a single one with a smile on the face. I turned to the Sister and I asked: "Why do these people, who have every—every comfort here, they are there looking toward the door? Why are they not smiling? I am so used to seeing the smiles on our people, even the dying ones' smile." And Sister said: "This is the way it is nearly every day. They are expecting, they are hoping that a son or a daughter will come to visit them. They are hurt because they are forgotten."

And see, this neglect to love brings spiritual poverty. Maybe in our own family we have somebody who is feeling lonely, who is feeling sick, who is feeling worried. Are we there? Are we willing to give until it hurts in order to be with our family, or do we put our interests first? These are the questions we must ask ourselves, especially as we begin this year of the family. We must remember that love begins at home. And we must also remember that: The future of humanity passes through the family.

I was surprised in the West to see so many young boys and girls given to drugs. And I tried to find out why. Why is it like that, when those in the West have so many more things than those in the East? And the answer was: because there is no one in the family to receive them. Our children depend on us for everything—their health, their nutrition, their security, their coming to know and love God. For all of this, they look to us with trust, hope, and expectation. But often father and mother are so busy they have no time for their children, or perhaps they are not even married or have given up on their marriage. So their children go to the streets and get involved in drugs or other things. We are talking of love of the child, which is where love and peace must begin—there, in our own family.

But I feel that the greatest destroyer of peace today is abortion, because Jesus said, "If you receive a little child, you receive me" [Mark 9:37]. So, every abortion is the denial of receiving Jesus—is the neglect of receiving Jesus.

It is really a war against the child, a direct killing of the innocent child, murder by the mother herself. And if we accept that a mother can kill even her own child, how can we tell other people not to kill one another? How do we persuade a woman not to have an abortion? As always, we must persuade her with love and we remind ourselves that love means to be willing to give until it hurts.

Jesus gave even His life to love us. So, the mother who is thinking of abortion should be helped to love—that is, to give until it hurts her plans, her free time, to respect the life of her child. For the child is the greatest gift of God to the family because they have been created to love and be loved.

The father of that child, however, must also give until it hurts.

By abortion, the mother does not learn to love, but kills even her own child to solve her problems. And, by abortion, the father is told that he does not have to take any responsibility at all for the child he has brought into the world. That…so that father is likely to put other women into the same trouble. So, abortion just leads to more abortion. Any country that accepts abortion is not teaching its people to love one another, but to use any violence to get what they want. This is why the greatest destroyer of love and peace is abortion.

The beautiful gift God has given our congregation is to fight abortion by adoption. We have given already…we have given already from one house in Calcutta, over 3,000 children in adoption. And I can't tell you what joy, what love, what peace those children have brought into those families. It has been a real gift of God for them and for us. I remember one of the little ones got very sick, so I sent for the father and the mother and I asked them: "Please give me back the sick child. I will give you a healthy one." And the father looked at me and said, "Mother Teresa, take my life first—then take the child." So beautiful to see it. So much love, so much joy that little one has brought into that family. So pray for us that we continue this beautiful gift. And also I offer you, since our Sisters are here, anybody who doesn't want the child, please give it to me. I…I want the child.

I will tell you something beautiful. As I already told you, the abortion by adoption—by care of the mother and adoption for her baby. We have saved thousands of lives. We have sent word to the clinics, to the hospitals and police stations: "Please don't destroy the child. We will take the child." So we always have someone tell the mothers in trouble: "Come, we will take…take care of you. We will get a home for your child." And we have a tremendous demand from couples who cannot have a child. But I never give a child to a couple who have done something not to have a child. Jesus said, "Anyone who receives a child in my name, receives me." By adopting a child, these couples receive Jesus but, by aborting a child, a couple refuses to receive Jesus.

Please don't kill the child. I want the child. Please give me the child. I am willing to accept any child who would be aborted and to give that child to [a] married couple who will love the child and be loved by the child.

I know that couples have to plan their family and for that there is natural family planning. The way to plan the family is natural family planning, not contraception. In destroying the power of giving life, of loving, through contraception, a husband or wife is doing something to self. This turns the attention to self, and so it destroys the gifts of love in him and her.

In loving, the husband and wife must turn the attention to each other, as happen[s] in natural family planning, and not to self, as happens in contraception. Once that living love is destroyed by contraception, abortion follows very easily. That's why I never give a child to a family that has used contraception, because if the mother has destroyed the power of loving, how will she love my child?

I also know that there are great problems in the world, that many spouses do not love each other enough to practice [natural family planning]. We cannot solve [all] the problems in the world, but let us never bring in the worst problem of all: to destroy love, to destroy life. The poor are very great people. They can teach us so many beautiful things. Once, one of them came to thank us for teaching her natural family planning and said: "You people who have practiced chastity, you are the best people to teach us natural family planning because it is nothing more than self-control out of love for each other." And what this poor person said is very true. These poor people maybe have nothing to eat, maybe…maybe they have not a home to live in, but they can still be great people when they are spiritually rich and love one another as God loves each one of them.

When I pick up a person from the streets, hungry, I give him a plate of rice, a piece of bread. But a person who is shut out, who feels unwanted, unloved, terrified, the person who has been thrown out of society—that spiritual poverty is much harder to be overcome. And abortion, which often follows from contraception, brings a people to be spiritually poor, and that is the worst poverty and the most difficult to overcome.

Those who are materially poor can be very wonderful people. One evening we went out and we picked up four people from the street.

And one of them was in a most terrible condition. I told the Sisters: "You take care of the other three; I will take care of the one who looks are worse." So I did for her all that my love can do. I put her in bed, and there was such a beautiful smile on her face. She took hold of my hand, as she said one word only: "Thank you." And she died.

I couldn't help but examine my conscience before her. And I asked: "What would I say if I were in her place?" And my answer was very simple. I would have tried to draw a little attention to myself. I would have said: "I am hungry. I am dying. I am cold. I am in pain." But she gave me much more: She gave me her grateful love. She died with a big smile on her face. Then there was the man we picked up from the drain, half eaten with worms. And after we had brought him to the home, he only said, "I have lived like an animal in the street, but I am going to die as an angel, loved and cared." Then, after we had removed all the worms from his body, all he said, with a big smile: "Sister, I am going home to God." And he died. I[t] was…was so wonderful to see the greatness of that man who could speak like that without blaming anybody, without comparing anything, like an angel. This is the greatness of people who are spiritually rich even when they are materially poor.

We are not social workers. We may be doing social work in the eyes of some people, but we must be contemplatives in the heart of the world. For we must bring that presence of God into your family. For the family that prays together, stays together. There is so much hatred, so much misery, and we with our prayer, with our sacrifice, are beginning at home. Love begins at home, and it is not how much we do, but how much love we put into what we do.

If we are contemplatives in the heart of the world with all its problem[s], these problems can never…discourage us. We must always remember that God tells us in Scripture: "Even if a mother could forget the child in her womb"—something impossible, but even if she could forget—"I will never forget you" [Isaiah 49:15].

And so, here I am talking with you. I want you to find the poor here, right in your own home first. And begin love there. Be that good news to your own people first. And find out about your next-door neighbor. Do you know who they are?

I had the most extraordinary experience of love of neighbor with a Hindu family. A gentleman came to our house and said: "Mother Teresa, there is a family who have not eaten for so long. Do something." So I took some rice and went there immediately. And I saw the children, their eyes shining with hunger. I don't know if you have ever seen hunger. But I have seen it very often. And the mother of the family took the rice I gave her and went out. When she came back, I asked her: "Where did you go? What did you do?" And she gave me a very simple answer: "They are hungry also."

What struck me was that she knew. And who [were they]? A Muslim family. And she knew that they were hungry. And I did not bring any more rice that evening because I wanted them, Hindus and family and Muslim family, to enjoy the joy of loving each other. She just left her own children, who were hungry; her first thought was her neighbor. But there were those children, radiating joy, sharing the joy and peace of their mother because she had the love to give until it hurts. And you see this is where love begins—at home in the family.

So, as the example of this family shows, God will never forget us, and there is something you and I can always do. We can keep the joy of loving Jesus in our hearts, and share that joy with all we come in contact with. Let us make that one point: that no child will be unwanted, unloved, uncared for, or killed and thrown away. And give until it hurts, with a smile. As you know, we have homes, a number of homes here in the United States, where people need tender love and care. This is the joy of sharing. Come and share. We have the young people suffering with AIDS. They need that tender love and care. But such beautiful smile I've never yet seen a young man or anybody, displeased or angry or frightened, really going home to God. Such a beautiful smile, always. So let us pray that we have the gift of sharing the joy with others and loving until it hurts.

Because I talk so much of giving with a smile, once a professor from the United States asked me: "Are you married?" And I said: "Yes, and I find it sometimes very difficult to smile at my spouse, Jesus, because He can be...He can be very demanding sometimes." This is really something true. And [this] is where love comes in: when it is demanding, and yet we can give it with joy.

One of the most demanding things for me is travelling everywhere—and with publicity. I have said to Jesus that if I don't go to heaven for anything else, I will be going to heaven for all the travelling with all the publicity, because it has purified me and sacrificed me and made me really ready to go home to God.

If we remember that God loves us, and that we can love others as He loves us, then America can become a sign of peace for the whole world, be a sign of joy. From here, a sign of care for the weakest [of] the weak, the unborn child, must go out to the world. If you become a burning light of justice and peace in the world, then really you will be true to what the founders…founders of this country stood for.

Let us love one another as God loves each one of us.

And where does this love begin? In our own home.

How does it begin? By praying together.

Pray for us that we continue God's work with great love. The sisters, the brothers, and the fathers, lay missionaries of Charity, and coworkers: We are all one heart full of love, that we may bring that joy of loving everywhere we go.

And my…my prayer for you is that through this love for one another, for this peace and joy in the family, that you may grow in holiness. Holiness is not the luxury of the few; it is a simply duty, for you and for me, because Jesus has very clearly said, "Be ye holy as the father in heaven is holy." So let us pray for each other that we grow in love for each other, and through this love become holy, as Jesus wants us to be, for he died out of love for us.

One day, I met a lady who was dying of cancer in a most terrible condition. And I told her, I say, "You know, this terrible pain is only the kiss of Jesus, a sign that you have come so close to Jesus on the cross that he can kiss you." And she joined her hands together and said, "Mother Teresa, please tell Jesus to stop kissing me."

So pray for us that we continue God's work with great love. And I will pray for you—for all your…all your families.

And also I want to thank the families who have been so generous in giving their daughters to us to—to consecrate their life to Jesus by the vow of poverty, chastity, obedience, and by giving wholehearted, free service to the poorest of the poor. This is our fourth vow in our congregation. And we have a novitiate in San Francisco where we have many beautiful vocations who are wanting to give their whole life to Jesus in the service of the poorest of the poor. So, once more, I thank you for giving you children to God. And pray for us that we continue God's work with great love. God bless you all.

Dorothy Day (1897–1980)

"I really only love God as much as I love the person I love the least."

On May 1, 1933, during the height of the Great Depression, Dorothy Day distributed the first issue of *Catholic Worker* in New York City's Union Square. The newspaper told the heartbreaking stories of the poor. Thirty-two years later, on November 6, 1965, Day returned to Union Square to speak in support of five young men who burned their draft cards in protest of the Vietnam War. These events exemplify the work of Dorothy Day in her staunch Catholic faith and activism; she tirelessly worked for social justice, peace, and against institutional structures that kept people impoverished spiritually and materially.

Born into a middle-class family, Dorothy Day was an avid life-long reader and identified and empathized with the poor and suffering. Among other works, she read about the plight of the urban poor in books like Sinclair's *The Jungle* and those of Russian novelists Tolstoy and Dostoevsky. She attended college and became a journalist, supporting herself with her writing. Two influences changed her life: Roman Catholicism and Peter Maurin. A self-taught intellectual, Maurin became Day's mentor, teaching her about Catholic history and theology and his vision of "cult, culture and cultivation," where all persons could thrive and find God through meeting each other's physical needs, and develop their capacity for creativity and love.[5]

Day embraced and implemented this vision with the *Catholic Worker* newspaper dedicated to "...those sitting on park benches...huddling in shelters...who think there is no hope for the future."[6] This paper funded houses of hospitality welcoming homeless and destitute people to live and share their meager fare. To many, she became the conscience of the Catholic Church calling the church to work for a society on earth as it is in heaven.

While she was an active writer and activist, Day seldom spoke in public settings. In her journal that November 6, 1965, Day wrote: "Demonstration in Union Square. 5 draft card burners. A. J. Muste and I spoke. My first time in open air." [7] Her words show the unbroken thread of her religion and pacifism. Speaking as "one who is old," Day endorses the "courage of the young" to give up their freedom in civil disobedience against the war. Day calls on the ethics of Jesus to love our enemies (Matthew 5:44), overcome evil with good (Romans 12:21), love each other as we are first loved by God (I John 4:19) and lay down our lives for our friends (John 15:13).

In every way, Day echoes Maurin's vision for human dignity and peace. Listing human achievements in space, health, and the success of non-violent liberation movements, Day applauds the struggles against war. She closes with the prayer of St. Francis of Assisi "Make me an instrument of your peace."

* * *

"Union Square Speech" (1965)[8]

New York City

November 6, 1965

When Jesus walked this earth; True God and True man, and was talking to the multitudes, a woman in the crowd cried out, "Blessed is the womb that bore you and the breast that nourished you." And he answered her, "Yes, but rather, blessed are those who hear the word of God and keep it."

And the word of God is the new commandment he gave us—to love our enemies, to overcome evil with good, to love others as he loved us—that is, to lay down our lives for our brothers throughout the world, not to take the lives of men, women, and children, young and old, by bombs and napalm and all the other instruments of war.

Instead he spoke of the instruments of peace, to be practiced by all nations—to feed the hungry of the world—not to destroy their crops, not to spend billions on defense, which means instruments of destruction. He commanded us to feed the hungry, shelter the homeless, to save lives, not to destroy them, these precious lives for whom he willingly sacrificed his own.

I speak today as one who is old, and who must uphold and endorse the courage of the young who themselves are willing to give up their freedom. I speak as one who is old, and whose whole lifetime has seen the cruelty and hysteria of war in this last half century. But who has also seen, praise God, the emerging nations of Africa and Asia, and Latin America, achieving in many instances their own freedom through non-violent struggles, side by side with violence. Our own country has through tens of thousands of the Negroe [sic] people, shown an example to the world of what a non-violent struggle can achieve. This very struggle, begun by students, by the young, by the seemingly helpless, have [sic]led the way in vision, in courage, even in a martyrdom, which has been shared by the little children, in the struggle for full freedom and for human dignity which means the right to health, education, and work which is a full development of man's God-given talents.

We have seen the works of man's genius and vision in the world today, in the conquering of space, in his struggle with plague and famine, and in each and every demonstration such as this one—there is evidence of his struggle against war.

I wish to place myself beside A. J. Muste speaking, if I am permitted, to show my solidarity of purpose with these young men, and to point out that we too are breaking the law, committing civil disobedience, in advocating and trying to encourage all those who are conscripted, to inform their conscience, to heed the still small voice, and to refuse to participate in the immorality of war. It is the most potent way to end war.

We too, by law, myself and all who signed the statement of conscience, should be arrested and we would esteem it an honor to share prison penalties with these others. I would like to conclude these few words with a prayer in the words of St. Francis, saint of poverty and peace, "O Lord, make me an instrument of your peace, / Where there is hatred, let me sow love."

Aung San Suu Kyi (1945–)

"To be kind is to respond with sensitivity and human warmth to the hopes and needs of others. Even the briefest touch of kindness can lighten a heavy heart."[9]

Affectionately known as "The Lady" to her people, Aung San Suu Kyi is an international symbol of peace, democracy, and non-violent protest in the spirit of Mahatma Gandhi. Her father, Aung San, was a leader in Burma's quest for liberation and was murdered when she was only two years old. Aung San Suu Kyi received her education at Oxford University, married, raised a family, and worked for the United Nations. She returned to Burma (now Myanmar) to care for her ailing mother in 1988, just as another Burmese revolt occurred. Aung San Suu Kyi emerged as the leader for the move for greater freedom, founded a political party, and gained political victory in 1990. However, the military refused to recognize the election results and placed her under house arrest from 1989 to 2010. Aung San Suu Kyi, separated from her family (the government would not allow visas), last saw her husband in 1995 before he died of cancer in 1999. She remained in her country because she refused to cede power to the military.

In 1991, the Nobel Committee awarded Aung San Suu Kyi the Peace Prize for "her unflagging efforts and to show its support for the many people throughout the world who are striving to attain democracy, human rights and ethnic conciliation by peaceful means."[10] Released from house arrest in 2010, she rose once again in leadership, and was elected to the Burmese Union Parliament in 2012. She is, however, constitutionally barred from presidential election. Since 2016, Aung San Suu Kyi has served as state counsellor, which is akin to being prime minister.

In 2012, Aung San Suu Kyi gave her Nobel Acceptance Speech, twenty-one years after its award. Here she speaks of her views of peace, ability to persevere under house arrest, and her Buddhist values. She recounts how she felt to be nominated while being confined to her home. Aung San Suu Kyi defines her understanding of peace as "the happiness arising from the cessation of factors that militate against the harmonious and the wholesome."

Mentioning the waste of young life during World War I, she asks if we are not all a bit reckless with humanity's future. "Wherever suffering is ignored, there will be the seeds of conflict, for suffering degrades and embitters and enrages." While under long house arrest, Aung San Suu Kyi contemplated the six kinds of suffering (*dukkha*) Buddha taught as part of the human condition and applied these to everyday life. This suffering includes: "to be conceived, to age, to sicken, to die, to be parted from those one loves, to be forced to live in propinquity with those one does not love." Applying these ideas to everyday life, the speaker reflects on the fate of those living in prison, refugee camps, or oppressed under repressive governments. She takes hope in the Universal Declaration of Human Rights.

Aung San Suu Kyi concedes that perfect peace is elusive; however, kindness is an important virtue. "To be kind," she tells us, "is to respond with sensitivity and human warmth to the hopes and needs of others." She urges all her hearers to work for a more peaceful world "where all can sleep in security and wake in happiness." The Lady's lifelong sacrifice and leadership for the Burmese people and the world encourages us toward compassion and kindness.

* * *

"Nobel Acceptance Speech" (2012)[11]

Oslo City Hall

June 16, 2012

Your Majesties, Your Royal Highness, Excellencies, Distinguished members of the Norwegian Nobel Committee, Dear Friends,

Long years ago, sometimes it seems many lives ago, I was at Oxford listening to the radio programme[12] *Desert Island Discs* with my young son Alexander. It was a well-known programme (for all I know it still continues) on which famous people from all walks of life were invited to talk about the eight discs, the one book beside the bible and the complete works of Shakespeare, and the one luxury item they would wish to have with them were they to be marooned on a desert island. At the end of the programme, which we had both enjoyed, Alexander asked me if I thought I might ever be invited to speak on *Desert Island Discs*. "Why not?" I responded lightly. Since he knew that in general only celebrities took part in the programme he proceeded to ask, with genuine interest, for what reason I thought I might be invited. I considered this for a moment and then answered: "Perhaps because I'd have won the Nobel Prize for literature," and we both laughed. The prospect seemed pleasant but hardly probable.

(I cannot now remember why I gave that answer, perhaps because I had recently read a book by a Nobel Laureate or perhaps because the *Desert Island* celebrity of that day had been a famous writer.)

In 1989, when my late husband Michael Aris came to see me during my first term of house arrest, he told me that a friend, John Finnis, had nominated me for the Nobel Peace Prize. This time also I laughed. For an instant Michael looked amazed, then he realized why I was amused. The Nobel Peace Prize? A pleasant prospect, but quite improbable! So how did I feel when I was actually awarded the Nobel Prize for Peace? The question has been put to me many times and this is surely the most appropriate occasion on which to examine what the Nobel Prize means to me and what peace means to me.

As I have said repeatedly in many an interview, I heard the news that I had been awarded the Nobel Peace Prize on the radio one evening. It did not altogether come as a surprise because I had been mentioned as one of the frontrunners for the prize in a number of broadcasts during the previous week. While drafting this lecture, I have tried very hard to remember what my immediate reaction to the announcement of the award had been. I think, I can no longer be sure, it was something like:

"Oh, so they've decided to give it to me." It did not seem quite real because in a sense I did not feel myself to be quite real at that time.

Often during my days of house arrest it felt as though I were no longer a part of the real world. There was the house which was my world, there was the world of others who also were not free but who were together in prison as a community, and there was the world of the free; each was a different planet pursuing its own separate course in an indifferent universe. What the Nobel Peace Prize did was to draw me once again into the world of other human beings outside the isolated area in which I lived, to restore a sense of reality to me. This did not happen instantly, of course, but as the days and months went by and news of reactions to the award came over the airwaves, I began to understand the significance of the Nobel Prize. It had made me real once again; it had drawn me back into the wider human community. And what was more important, the Nobel Prize had drawn the attention of the world to the struggle for democracy and human rights in Burma. We were not going to be forgotten.

To be forgotten. The French say that to part is to die a little. To be forgotten too is to die a little. It is to lose some of the links that anchor us to the rest of humanity. When I met Burmese migrant workers and refugees during my recent visit to Thailand, many cried out: "Don't forget us!" They meant: "don't forget our plight, don't forget to do what you can to help us, don't forget we also belong to your world." When the Nobel Committee awarded the Peace Prize to me they were recognizing that the oppressed and the isolated in Burma were also a part of the world, they were recognizing the oneness of humanity. So, for me receiving the Nobel Peace Prize means personally extending my concerns for democracy and human rights beyond national borders. The Nobel Peace Prize opened up a door in my heart.

The Burmese concept of peace can be explained as the happiness arising from the cessation of factors that militate against the harmonious and the wholesome. The word *nyein-chan* translates literally as the beneficial coolness that comes when a fire is extinguished. Fires of suffering and strife are raging around the world. In my own country, hostilities have not ceased in the far north; to the west, communal violence resulting in arson and murder were taking place just several days before I started out on the journey that has brought me here today. News of atrocities in other reaches of the earth abound. Reports of hunger, disease, displacement, joblessness, poverty, injustice, discrimination, prejudice, bigotry; these are our daily fare. Everywhere there are negative forces eating away at the foundations of peace. Everywhere can be found thoughtless dissipation of material and human resources that are necessary for the conservation of harmony and happiness in our world.

The First World War represented a terrifying waste of youth and potential, a cruel squandering of the positive forces of our planet. The poetry of that era has a special significance for me because I first read it at a time when I was the same age as many of those young men who had to face the prospect of withering before they had barely blossomed. A young American fighting with the French Foreign Legion wrote before he was killed in action in 1916 that he would meet his death: "at some disputed barricade"; "on some scarred slope of battered hill"; "at midnight in some flaming town." Youth and love and life perishing forever in senseless attempts to capture nameless, unremembered places. And for what? Nearly a century on, we have yet to find a satisfactory answer.

Are we not still guilty, if to a less violent degree, of recklessness, of improvidence with regard to our future and our humanity? War is not the only arena where peace is done to death. Wherever suffering is ignored, there will be the seeds of conflict, for suffering degrades and embitters and enrages.

A positive aspect of living in isolation was that I had ample time in which to ruminate over the meaning of words and precepts that I had known and accepted all my life. As a Buddhist, I had heard about *dukha*, generally translated as suffering, since I was a small child. Almost on a daily basis elderly, and sometimes not so elderly, people around me would murmur "*dukha, dukha*" when they suffered from aches and pains or when they met with some small, annoying mishaps. However, it was only during my years of house arrest that I got around to investigating the nature of the six great *dukha*. These are: to be conceived, to age, to sicken, to die, to be parted from those one loves, to be forced to live in propinquity with those one does not love. I examined each of the six great sufferings, not in a religious context but in the context of our ordinary, everyday lives. If suffering were an unavoidable part of our existence, we should try to alleviate it as far as possible in practical, earthly ways. I mulled over the effectiveness of ante- and post-natal programmes and mother and childcare; of adequate facilities for the aging population; of comprehensive health services; of compassionate nursing and hospices. I was particularly intrigued by the last two kinds of suffering: to be parted from those one loves and to be forced to live in propinquity with those one does not love. What experiences might our Lord Buddha have undergone in his own life that he had included these two states among the great sufferings? I thought of prisoners and refugees, of migrant workers and victims of human trafficking, of that great mass of the uprooted of the earth who have been torn away from their homes, parted from families and friends, forced to live out their lives among strangers who are not always welcoming.

We are fortunate to be living in an age when social welfare and humanitarian assistance are recognized not only as desirable but necessary. I am fortunate to be living in an age when the fate of prisoners of conscience anywhere has become the concern of peoples everywhere, an age when democracy and human rights are widely, even if not universally, accepted as the birthright of all. How often during my years under house arrest have I drawn strength from my favourite passages in the preamble to the Universal Declaration of Human Rights:

> "...disregard and contempt for human rights have resulted in barbarous acts which have outraged the conscience of mankind, and the advent of a world in which human beings shall enjoy freedom of speech and belief and freedom from fear and want has been proclaimed as the highest aspirations of the common people...it is essential, if man is not to be compelled to have recourse, as a last resort, to rebellion against tyranny and oppression, that human rights should be protected by the rule of law..."

If I am asked why I am fighting for human rights in Burma the above passages will provide the answer. If I am asked why I am fighting for democracy in Burma, it is because I believe that democratic institutions and practices are necessary for the guarantee of human rights.

Over the past year there have been signs that the endeavours of those who believe in democracy and human rights are beginning to bear fruit in Burma. There have been changes in a positive direction; steps towards democratization have been taken. If I advocate cautious optimism it is not because I do not have faith in the future but because I do not want to encourage blind faith. Without faith in the future, without the conviction that democratic values and fundamental human rights are not only necessary but possible for our society, our movement could not have been sustained throughout the destroying years. Some of our warriors fell at their post, some deserted us, but a dedicated core remained strong and committed.

At times when I think of the years that have passed, I am amazed that so many remained staunch under the most trying circumstances. Their faith in our cause is not blind; it is based on a clear-eyed assessment of their own powers of endurance and a profound respect for the aspirations of our people.

It is because of recent changes in my country that I am with you today; and these changes have come about because of you and other lovers of freedom and justice who contributed towards a global awareness of our situation. Before continuing to speak of my country, may I speak out for our prisoners of conscience. There still remain such prisoners in Burma. It is to be feared that because the best-known detainees have been released, the remainder, the unknown ones, will be forgotten. I am standing here because I was once a prisoner of conscience. As you look at me and listen to me, please remember the often repeated truth that one prisoner of conscience is one too many. Those who have not yet been freed, those who have not yet been given access to the benefits of justice in my country number much more than one. Please remember them and do whatever is possible to affect their earliest, unconditional release.

Burma is a country of many ethnic nationalities and faith in its future can be founded only on a true spirit of union. Since we achieved independence in 1948, there never has been a time when we could claim the whole country was at peace. We have not been able to develop the trust and understanding necessary to remove causes of conflict. Hopes were raised by ceasefires that were maintained from the early 1990s until 2010 when these broke down over the course of a few months. One unconsidered move can be enough to remove long-standing ceasefires. In recent months, negotiations between the government and ethnic nationality forces have been making progress. We hope that ceasefire agreements will lead to political settlements founded on the aspirations of the peoples, and the spirit of union.

My party, the National League for Democracy, and I stand ready and willing to play any role in the process of national reconciliation. The reform measures that were put into motion by President U Thein Sein's government can be sustained only with the intelligent coopera-tion of all internal forces: the military, our ethnic nationalities, political parties, the media, civil society organizations, the business commu-nity and, most important of all, the general public. We can say that reform is effective only if the lives of the people are improved and in this regard, the international community has a vital role to play. Devel-opment and humanitarian aid, bi-lateral agreements and investments should be coordinated and calibrated to ensure that these will promote social, political and economic growth that is balanced and sustainable. The potential of our country is enormous. This should be nurtured and developed to create not just a more prosperous but also a more harmo-nious, democratic society where our people can live in peace, security and freedom.

The peace of our world is indivisible. As long as negative forces are getting the better of positive forces anywhere, we are all at risk. It may be questioned whether all negative forces could ever be removed. The simple answer is: "No!" It is in human nature to contain both the positive and the negative. However, it is also within human capabil-ity to work to reinforce the positive and to minimize or neutralize the negative. Absolute peace in our world is an unattainable goal. But it is one towards which we must continue to journey, our eyes fixed on it as a traveller in a desert fixes his eyes on the one guiding star that will lead him to salvation. Even if we do not achieve perfect peace on earth, because perfect peace is not of this earth, common endeavours to gain peace will unite individuals and nations in trust and friendship and help to make our human community safer and kinder.

I used the word 'kinder' after careful deliberation; I might say the careful deliberation of many years. Of the sweets of adversity, and let me say that these are not numerous, I have found the sweetest, the most precious of all, is the lesson I learnt on the value of kindness. Every kindness I received, small or big, convinced me that there could never be enough of it in our world. To be kind is to respond with sensitivity and human warmth to the hopes and needs of others. Even the briefest touch of kindness can lighten a heavy heart. Kindness can change the lives of people. Norway has shown exemplary kindness in providing a home for the displaced of the earth, offering sanctuary to those who have been cut loose from the moorings of security and freedom in their native lands.

There are refugees in all parts of the world. When I was at the Maela refugee camp in Thailand recently, I met dedicated people who were striving daily to make the lives of the inmates as free from hardship as possible. They spoke of their concern over 'donor fatigue,' which could also translate as 'compassion fatigue.' 'Donor fatigue' expresses itself precisely in the reduction of funding. 'Compassion fatigue' expresses itself less obviously in the reduction of concern. One is the consequence of the other. Can we afford to indulge in compassion fatigue? Is the cost of meeting the needs of refugees greater than the cost that would be consequent on turning an indifferent, if not a blind, eye on their suffering? I appeal to donors the world over to fulfill the needs of these people who are in search, often it must seem to them a vain search, of refuge.

At Maela, I had valuable discussions with Thai officials responsible for the administration of Tak province where this and several other camps are situated. They acquainted me with some of the more serious problems related to refugee camps: violation of forestry laws, illegal drug use, home brewed spirits, the problems of controlling malaria, tuberculosis, dengue fever and cholera. The concerns of the administration are as legitimate as the concerns of the refugees. Host countries also deserve consideration and practical help in coping with the difficulties related to their responsibilities.

Ultimately our aim should be to create a world free from the displaced, the homeless and the hopeless, a world of which each and every corner is a true sanctuary where the inhabitants will have the freedom and the capacity to live in peace. Every thought, every word, and every action that adds to the positive and the wholesome is a contribution to peace. Each and every one of us is capable of making such a contribution. Let us join hands to try to create a peaceful world where we can sleep in security and wake in happiness.

The Nobel Committee concluded its statement of 14 October 1991 with the words: "In awarding the Nobel Peace Prize…to Aung San Suu Kyi, the Norwegian Nobel Committee wishes to honour this woman for her unflagging efforts and to show its support for the many people throughout the world who are striving to attain democracy, human rights and ethnic conciliation by peaceful means." When I joined the democracy movement in Burma it never occurred to me that I might ever be the recipient of any prize or honour. The prize we were working for was a free, secure and just society where our people might be able to realize their full potential. The honour lay in our endeavour. History had given us the opportunity to give of our best for a cause in which we believed. When the Nobel Committee chose to honour me, the road I had chosen of my own free will became a less lonely path to follow. For this I thank the Committee, the people of Norway and peoples all over the world whose support has strengthened my faith in the common quest for peace. Thank you.

Notes

1 Mae Elise Cannon, *Just Spirituality: How Faith Practices Fuel Social Action* (Downers Grove, IL: InterVarsity Press, 2013), 19.

2 Malcolm Muggeridge, *Something Beautiful for God: Mother Teresa of Calcutta* (Garden City, NY: Image Books, 1977), 22.

3 See Christopher Hitchens' *The Missionary Position: Mother Teresa in Theory and Practice* (London: Verso, 1995) as a primary critique of Mother Teresa and her work.

4   The writings of Mother Teresa of Calcutta © by the Mother Teresa Center, exclu-
    sive licensee throughout the world of the Missionaries of Charity for the works of
    Mother Teresa. Used with permission.

5   Dorothy Day, *The Long Loneliness: The Autobiography of the Legendary Catholic Social
    Activist* (New York NY: Harper & Row, 1952), 171.

6   Dorothy Day and Robert Ellsberg, *The Duty of Delight: The Diaries of Dorothy Day*
    (New York NY: Image Books, 2011), xv.

7   Ibid., 383. A. J. Muste was a Christian pacifist and civil rights activist whose ideas
    inspired Day to her Christian activism. His teaching and thinking informed many
    of her politics and practices.

8   Dorothy Day, "Union Square Speech" (speech, Union Square, New York City, New
    York, November 6, 1975), Voices of Democracy, accessed March 1, 2018, http://
    voicesofdemocracy.umd.edu/day-union-square-speech-speech-text/

9   Aung San Suu Kyi, *Freedom from Fear and Other Writings* (London: Penguin Books,
    1991), 236–237.

10 Aung San Suu Kyi, *Freedom from Fear and Other Writings* (London: Penguin Books,
    1991), 236–237.

11 Aung San Suu Kyi. "Nobel Lecture" (speech, Oslo City Hall, Oslo, Norway, June
    16, 2012), Nobel Media AB, accessed February 17, 2017, http://www.nobelprize.
    org/nobel_prizes/peace/laureates/1991/kyi-lecture_en.html

12 Due to the location of the speech and the source of the transcript, British-English
    spellings are preserved throughout the text.

Conclusion

What can we take away as we leave this collection of women's voices? In full recognition that other worthy speakers and speeches could and should be studied, what wisdom does this sampler offer? This is largely up to the reader to decide, of course, but as we move forward, here are a few parting thoughts.

Throughout this book, I have made connections between the dialectical tensions of the backward pull of *duty* to conform to proscribed women's roles and place, and the push forward toward *destiny* and human freedom, as influenced by religious values. Every speaker and address represented in this book, in effect, has attempted to reconcile these tensions in the life and rhetorical choices each has made. Every speaker is a leader, some overcoming great hardship, and each diligent in hard work in service of others in her given sphere of influence. These orators are exemplars of servant leadership in partnership with a freeing vision of the divine.

In addition, I have referred to the narrative paradigm to consider the larger story each speaker is inviting the audience to join in her proposal for change. Using the skills of story-telling, each speaker has endeavored to persuade her audiences to live by the transcendent values of their shared discourse communities. Rabbi Sally J. Priesand and Agnes Baker Pilgrim each articulated the importance of repairing and replenishing the world around us in partnership with the divine.

Clarina Howard Nichols, Phyllis Schlafly, and Elizabeth Cady Stanton share very different views on women's societal roles and still connect these perspectives with the transcendent value of women's worth. What they communicate in common is how women must be given the necessary freedoms in law to carry out their responsibilities as individual persons and chosen societal roles in family and community. Nichols appeals to traditional roles; Schlafly calls for protection of the home; and Stanton names the solitude and responsibility for one's own life as the basis for all freedoms.

Maria W. Stewart and Mary McLeod Bethune both proclaim the importance of education to human flourishing and prosperity. Their call for equal access to educational opportunities for all people connects their Christian belief that humans share the divine image and assertion that the United States must make a way forward for all citizens to reach their full potential in the pursuit of knowledge.

It is unconscionable for one human being to enslave another for any purpose proclaim both Sojourner Truth and Dr. Brook Bello in their calls for their audiences to rise up against slavery of every kind. Both invoke their discourse communities' transcendent values of human freedom and equality as confirmed by the examples of their own lives and advocacy on behalf of others.

Frances E. Willard and Aimee Semple McPherson each grew beyond the duty of convention to conform to social roles and became extraordinary examples of overcoming gender stereotypes in their respective worlds. Willard, an educator and then advocate for abstinence from alcohol, led the most successful women's movement of her time. The impulse to make a better world in "home protection" expresses her belief in the transcendent ideal of family and community. McPherson, on the other hand, recognizes the foibles of humanity, and, despite many controversies, founded both a denomination and megachurch.

Finally, in their dissimilar visions of how to make a more peaceful world, Mother Teresa, Dorothy Day, and Aung San Suu Kyi each address the values she holds most dear. For Mother Teresa, her religious values call for a commitment to life at every level from the unborn child to the dying elder. She states that the way the weakest in a society are ill-treated is the essential cause for violence. Day, in contrast, dedicated her life to serving the poor in social justice activism though food, housing, employment, journalism, and politics and proposes a commitment to radical pacifism. Finally, "The Lady," Aung Sun Suu Kyi recognizes the complexities involved in efforts for global peacemaking but proposes that simple human kindness is a good place to begin.

As a final thought, it is important to note that each of these speakers, and we as audience members, are all flawed human beings. There is a current trend to judge historic perspectives from the light of today's politics and ideology. I propose that a closer examination of each speaker, her audience, discourse communities, time, religious, and cultural contexts can guide us to a better understanding. We might ourselves appreciate this grace as our lives and words are judged by the future.

Perhaps, we can consider the transcendent values of honoring the earth, accepting our freedoms and responsibility within society, pursuing knowledge and wisdom, freeing people from bondage, serving the common good, and making peace with all people, as the embodiment of religious faith. While these women each bear her individual witness to her issues and times, between the call of duty and destiny, each is a woman created in the divine image.

Speaking of Religion

Daniel S. Brown, *Series Editor*

Speaking of Religion grows from a scholarly attentiveness to the role that religion plays in the public sphere. The decline of religious thought in public affairs is a common yet false narrative in the United States. Americans remain a devout people who are motivated to action by their faith commitments. Several contemporary, interdisciplinary scholars including Jürgen Habermas, Charles Taylor and Tariq Ramadan point us toward the privilege that religion and faith enjoys in public life. Collectively their work asserts that the world has entered a post-secular era: Secularism is dead and faith is alive. *Speaking of Religion* features short books, no more than 60,000 words or approximately 150 pages in length.

For additional information about this series or for the submission of manuscripts, please contact:

Peter Lang Publishing
Acquisitions Department
29 Broadway, 18th floor
New York, NY 10006

To order books in this series, please contact our Customer Service Department:

800-770-LANG (within the U.S.)
212-647-7706 (outside the U.S.)
212-647-7707 FAX

Or browse online by series at:

www.peterlang.com